OLD DOG, NEW TRICKS'

THE POWER OF LEADING WITH EMOTIONAL INTELLIGENCE

I0517766

DR. BARRY DAVIS

ISBN: 978-1-956464-63-4

First Edition 2025

This publication is intended to provide accurate information on the subject matter covered. It is sold with the understanding that neither the author nor the publisher offers legal, investment, accounting, medical, or other professional advice. The author and publisher make no representations or warranties regarding the accuracy or completeness of the contents and expressly disclaim any implied warranties of merchantability or fitness for a particular purpose. No warranties may be extended by sales representatives or materials. Professional consultation is recommended as individual circumstances vary. Neither the author nor the publisher shall be liable for any damages, including but not limited to loss of profit, incidental, or consequential damages.

Published by BrightRay Publishing
https://brightray.com/

To Dad,

You never pushed—you guided.
Sports, and ultimately coaching,
became my life's work because of you.
Thank you.

Praise for
OLD DOG, NEW TRICKS

"*Old Dog, New Tricks* is a powerful guide that seamlessly blends leadership principles with life-changing lessons. It offers practical insights on how to lead yourself and others through personal transformation. With every page, Coach Davis encourages readers to embrace change, face challenges with resilience, and become the best version of themselves."

—Harry Perretta, Former Villanova Women's
Basketball Coach with 783 DI Career Wins

"*Old Dog, New Tricks* is an entertaining and practical reminder that great coaches 'coach people first, sport second.' Coach Davis draws on his wealth of experience leading teams to success and combines it with an in-depth study of coaching and leadership. The result is a unique book that I recommend to anyone who is serious about improving as a coach."

—Dr. Wade Gilbert, Coaching Scientist,
Performance Consultant, Author, and
Professor at Fresno State

"Davis has truly nailed it with *Old Dog, New Tricks*. As a coach, I've always known there's more to leadership than just strategy and X's and O's, but this book really takes it to another level. You'll walk away with real-world strategies and insights you can apply immediately. It's a must-buy for any coach or leader!"

—Jason Thompson, 8-Year NBA Player, 14-Year Pro, and Assistant Coach for the Sioux Falls Skyforce

"Coach Barry Davis had a profound impact on me as a young player. His professionalism inspired me to pursue a career in baseball. His book offers practical, actionable lessons that you can use to elevate your organization, your team, and your leadership."

—Dayton Moore, World Series Winning General Manager and Senior Advisor for the Texas Rangers

"*Old Dog, New Tricks* is a game-changer for leaders who aspire to cultivate a winning mindset and culture."

—Brian Cain, World-Renowned Expert in Mental Performance

"It's engaging, insightful, and a fun, easy read. It will make you look at your leadership style in a whole new way."

—Gary Gilmore, Head Baseball Coach at Coastal Carolina, 2016 NCAA DI National Champions

CONTENTS

FOREWORD, xi

PREFACE, xiii

PART I: BUILDING THE FOUNDATION, 1

1. Change and Acquire Talent, 2
2. Skilled but Flawed—
   Unconventional Wisdom, 7
3. Be Visible in the Community, 11
4. Philosophy Starts with Vision, 17
5. Great Company Wins, 22
6. What Do You Think?, 26
7. Attitude Determines Your Altitude, 31
8. Have Great Meetings, 37
9. Great Teams Have Great Leaders, 41
10. What Is a Lady Foxhound?, 48
11. Campus Connections, 53
12. Community Support, 57

Summary of Part I: Building the Foundation, 61

Part I References, 63

PART II: **PREPARATION**, 67

13. Set the Example, 68

14. The Green Line, 77

15. Praise, 81

16. Vulnerability, 86

17. Stop-Start-Continue, 91

18. First Impression, 95

19. I Need Two Solutions, 100

20. Filling Buckets, 105

21. Be a Level 10, 110

Summary of Part II: Preparation, 116

Part II References, 118

PART III: **THE SEASON BEGINS**, 121

22. Losing Is Learning, 122

23. Synergy and Grit, 129

24. The Standard Is the Standard, 133

25. Stories, 139

26. Managing Moments, 146

27. It's the Little Things, 154

28. David vs. Goliath, 160

29. Resolve, 165

30. MTA, 170

31. History and Winning Ugly, 174

Summary of Part III: The Season Begins, 180

Part III References, 182

PART IV: CONFERENCE SEASON, 185

32. Winners Never Quit, 186

33. Empathy, 194

34. Fighting Complacency, 199

35. Mental Imagery, 204

36. Kaizen, 209

Summary of Part IV: The Conference Season, 218

     A Summary on Emotional Intelligence, 220

Part IV References, 221

CONCLUSION, 223

ACKNOWLEDGMENTS, 225

ABOUT THE AUTHOR, 229

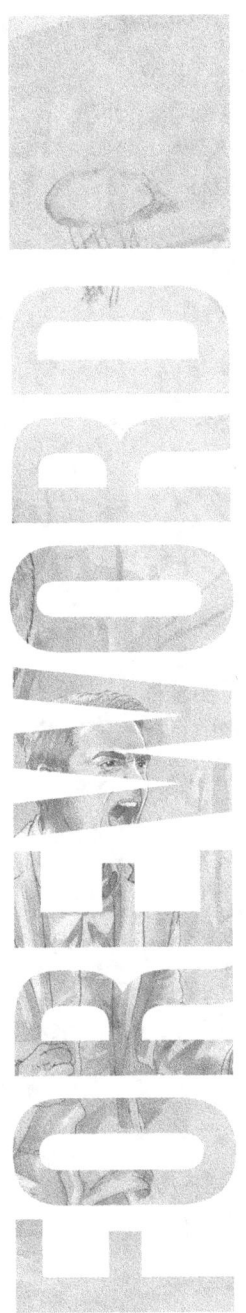

On January 29, 2025, Coach Barry Davis emailed me the manuscript for this book. Several hours later, I texted him: *"Coach, it's 3:30 a.m. Why am I still up? Because I cannot put your book down!"*

WARNING: The same thing is going to happen to you. *Old Dog, New Tricks* is un-put-down-able! Once you start reading it, you won't be able to stop. I read this entire book in less than a day. Did I like Coach Davis's book? NO, I LOVED IT!!!

In your hands, you have the best athletic leadership book ever written. If you're a coach, athletic director, or athletic administrator, this book is required reading.

I've always known Coach Davis is a great coach. His teams have won an amazing 1,054 games. I also know Dr. Davis is a smart guy. In fact, he's the only DI coach I'm aware of who has earned a PhD. What I didn't know is what a great writer and storyteller he is!

Here's what you can look forward to: *Old Dog, New Tricks* is *Hoosiers*— arguably the greatest sports movie of all time—meets *The One Minute Manager*, one of the best-selling leadership books.

One of the things that I loved most about this book was all the great leadership quotes. I want to add one of my own—a variation on a quote from Alexander the Great: "A team of lions led by a lamb will always lose to a team of lambs led by a lion." This quote is about powerful "lion-like" leadership. If you want to become a more powerful "lion-like" leader, *Old Dog, New Tricks* will definitely help you.

Here's your lion-leadership game plan:

1. Read *Old Dog, New Tricks*
2. Read *The One Minute Manager*
3. Watch *Hoosiers*

While you're doing your assignments, keep a list of the strategies you've discovered that will make you more of a "lion-like" leader. But, remember:

$$K - A = 0$$

Knowledge minus Action equals Zero

This means that if you know what to do but don't do what you know, it's meaningless. In other words, *implement* these strategies! If you do, I promise that you can expect a miracle!

Rob Gilbert, PhD
Professor at Montclair State University
Podcast Host of *Success Hotline*

My life changed on January 5th, 2007, in Orlando, Florida. Having been a collegiate head coach for 18 years, I surprisingly didn't associate the term "leadership" with myself. After all, I am a coach, not a leader—right? Wrong! Pat Williams, the vice president and general manager of the Orlando Magic, delivered a jaw-dropping speech on his seven sides of leadership. Walking out of the jam-packed conference room, it was evident that X's and O's were less important than leadership. And so, my leadership quest began.

This narrative is about two men who pull a struggling women's basketball program from rock bottom. One is a great leader and mentor, and the other is a great coach who needs the other to hone his emotional intelligence and self-control. Collectively, they implement a proven foundational philosophy to transform the program with the addition of unique and unconventional techniques. I encourage anyone heading up an athletic program or a struggling organization to read, reflect, and come up with ideas to adjust your philosophy to transform your team or organization.

Enjoy,

Coach Barry Davis, PhD

PART I
BUILDING THE FOUNDATION

CHANGE AND ACQUIRE TALENT

1

> *The greatest leader is not necessarily the one who does the greatest things. He is the one that gets the people to do the greatest things.*
>
> —Ronald Reagan,
> 40th President of the United States

As interest in women's college basketball exploded across America with unprecedented popularity, it was barely breathing at sleepy Virginia Central State University. A once proud VCSU program had hit rock bottom the prior season, finishing an embarrassing 3–27. There was a clear problem to be solved.

Each season brought a glimmer of hope, only to be extinguished by bad plays and even worse coaching. A deep sense of hopelessness and despair seeped into everyone associated with the program, and team pride was a distant memory.

These feelings were reflected in the program's poor attendance as fewer and fewer fans showed up to watch the Foxhounds. Most nights, less than 1000 fans trundled into Lewis and Clark Auditorium ("The Lewis"), which could seat 5,842, as the losses mounted. There was little to get excited about.

Over the past five years, the alumni base became more agitated with the rudderless direction of the program and had become increasingly unwilling to reach into their pockets to support the program, thinking it was a lost cause. Outside donations had plummeted too, and the push for change escalated. The program's stakeholders, who had once only suggested, were now *demanding* a new university president who could attract a proven winner as head coach.

Women's college basketball was thriving, and VCSU needed to hitch its wagon to the sport's growth. Tickets had reached never-before-seen prices. Most recently, women's Final Four ticket prices were double that of the men's Final Four.[1] University stakeholders wanted a piece of that action, and VCSU was missing out. It was time—the program needed to change. That change started when Dr. James Harding was announced as Virginia Central State's new president. He was the right person for the job; the board of trustees knew Harding as a leader with a well-established background in both academics and athletics. He was a sports fan and seemed to offer what the women's basketball program needed most: hope.

Harding got right to work by dismissing the athletic director and women's basketball coach within weeks of his presidency. His first challenge was to find dependable, capable replacements for each. Harding, confident in his ability to mentor, sought to hire the best candidates, provide them the freedom to turn the program around, and guide them—as needed—to ensure success.

Almost overnight, the atmosphere surrounding the women's basketball program shifted into high gear. Anticipation of a new coach gave all fans confidence that championships were soon on their way.

Dr. James Harding—Jimmy to his closest friends—was a former college basketball star at the University of Georgia in the mid-1980s. Not only was he a great player, he was also an Academic All-American. High school teachers and his parents had emphasized education. Jimmy had minored in history with a major in psychology. His IQ was high, but his people skills were even higher. He was an outlier among his peers, and when you met him, you knew why.

Jimmy stood 6-foot-2, 190 pounds, athletic, and looked as if he could still play even at 60. His hair, now peppered with gray, had thinned over the years. He was often simply dressed in a hemp-colored collared shirt, readers dangling around his neck, a brown leather belt holding up his khaki straight-legged chinos, black and tan leather-tasseled shoes, and no socks. His seemingly permanent five o'clock shadow added to his guise. He was the type of man that guys wanted to be, and there was something about Jimmy that drew people in—he was the perfect man for the job.

Harding brought nearly three decades of college experience to the presidency. He'd been a head coach at both the junior college and Division III levels and had won national championships at both. He later moved into athletic administration as an athletic director—hiring the right kind of people became an art form. He had innate skills that were difficult to duplicate. He quickly advanced after only five years, becoming a university provost. And after eight years working as a provost, Harding was ready to cap his career with only one job left to conquer: university president.

Harding's work ethic, along with his grit and persistence, left the rest of the field behind. Still, what truly set him apart were his people skills. A gold-medal people connector, the humble Harding made everyone feel important. He empowered his people, and in return, they excelled. His favorite question to ask was, "What do you think?" Then he'd sit back and wait for a response without interruption. But he didn't just hear— he *listened*. People often said that if you spoke with Jimmy long enough, he would know more about you than you knew about him. He always focused on others, purposely avoiding attention and deflecting glory in their direction. He would later say, "If I did such a great job, I would not need to talk about myself—others would do it for me."

Another skill that separated him from the pack was his ability to remain calm in the heat of the moment. A former player once said of Coach Harding, "No matter how crazy things got, he was never shook."

The board of trustees made it perfectly clear to Harding that he had one goal for the athletics department in his new role as university president: to resurrect and rebuild the women's basketball program. As a basketball fan who was also acutely aware of the growing phenomenon of the women's game, Harding knew the importance of hiring the right head coach. His decision was a surprise to everyone. The "right" person on his radar was the notorious Darren Blood.

🐾 Jimmy 🐾

Jimmy Harding knew the most important hire he'd make for any athletic program would be that of the head coach. Despite his jagged edges, Darren Blood was his first choice for the women's basketball team. It was an enormous risk, but one Harding believed was worth taking.

Darren Blood was Jimmy Harding's high school teammate, and those formative years together shaped Harding as a player. He later acknowledged this, noting, "I wouldn't have received a DI scholarship to Georgia if it weren't for my point guard, Darren Blood."

Jimmy, fully aware of Darren's abilities as well as his shortcomings, was following his instincts with this hire. *You have to trust what you feel is best. It can be risky, but the risk often leads to the greatest reward,* Jimmy reminded himself.

The new president successfully convinced the board of trustees to approve his choice for the new basketball coach, though Jimmy's passionate plea didn't entirely erase their doubts. These same doubts lingered with Jimmy as well. He had the sweaty palms, rising heartbeat, and slight tension headache to prove it. Jimmy, knowing he had burned his boats, had never second-guessed himself in the past, but the little man in his head was arguing persuasively that he'd made a mistake with Darren and had let his personal feelings for the hard-bitten coach influence his decision. But Jimmy refused to listen. His palms would remain sweaty for a little longer.

SKILLED BUT FLAWED—UNCONVENTIONAL WISDOM

> *Risk comes from not knowing what you're doing.*
>
> —Warren Buffett,
> Investor and Philanthropist

✎ Darren ✐

Darren Blood was a no-nonsense, unrelenting son of a bitch. He was the guy you wanted on your team but hated to play against. He loved all sports, but basketball grabbed his heart. So when he could no longer play, coaching became the next best thing. He deeply cherished competition, strategy, and the grind. It was his life's work. He loved to win. Losing nearly killed him. For Darren, basketball was more than a game, and coaching was more than a profession; it was his obsession.

Hired as head coach of the New York Knicks at the age of 37, Darren was a phenom. At 42, he won an NBA championship. Darren was known for his ability to strategize and teach the game; however, his mastery as a coach ended there. Off the court, he lacked people skills, had little self-awareness and even less self-control, and hardly ever listened to anything other than the sound of his own voice. He rarely gave praise, frequently criticized others publicly, and didn't know how to empower people. Darren's micromanagement style left his assistants feeling unappreciated and undervalued—not ideal for a cohesive coaching staff. Even his players came to hate him. One former player said, "It was a living hell just being near him."

Darren's uncontrollable behavior and insatiable desire to win, which worsened with each season, finally reached a breaking point one Christmas Day. In front of a sold-out Madison Square—and millions more at home—he lost his mind entirely, attacking a referee. While the fight was quickly broken up, Darren walked away from the game in disgrace. The scandal compounded when, later that same night, he lost control of his SUV in a single-car accident. He was arrested and charged with reckless driving as well as a DUI. Darren spent the night in jail and was fired the next day.

Okaloosa-Walton Junior College (now Northwest Florida State College) gave him a second chance, but Darren's downward spiral continued. He was fired less than 365 days after taking the job. He verbally abused his players and his staff, creating a toxic culture. Coach Blood was soon removed, and this second firing placed him on an unofficial blacklist.

Darren spent the next decade trying to return to the game he loved, but he couldn't keep his drinking or his temper in check, and with his checkered past, he wasn't on any pro team or college program's shortlist.

Sportswriters and critics like Gene Hack were quick to comment. The longtime New York sports columnist wrote, "Darren Blood is a disgrace to the profession. His teams quit on him. His courtside demeanor is embarrassing. How he still calls himself a coach is beyond me."

No one was willing to take a chance on a coach who, in many people's eyes, had zero emotional control, zero people skills, and, at best, a rigid old-school mindset.

Darren knew he had to change. There was no choice. He prayed. He begged the heavens to give him one more shot at the sport he had dedicated his life to. The universe obliged when his friend, Jimmy Harding, came calling.

It was a mid-August morning, late in college basketball circles, when Darren's phone buzzed. It was a text. *"Jimmy here. Call me when you get a chance. I have good news."*

Darren thought, *What in the world could he want?*

Nervous, Darren pulled up Jimmy's number and gave him a call. "What's up, Jimmy? It's been a long time, buddy. Where are you now?" Last Darren knew, Jimmy was acting provost of some university.

"I was just named the new president at Virginia Central . . . You know, VCSU."

"Really! Yeah, I've heard of the place. So what's up? Whatcha need?"

"I need a new head coach for women's basketball. And I want you to fill the position."

Darren nearly dropped the phone in surprise. *Women's basketball? He'd never coached women before. But still, it **was** a head coach position . . .*

"Really? Why me? . . . Are you sure you want me?" Darren's words seemed to catch in his throat.

Jimmy chuckled. "Yeah, you. So, Darren, are you interested in the job or what?"

Silence.

"Darren? You still there?"

"Still here, Harding," Darren said. "I'm just thinking through my options."

"Options? What options? You have none," Jimmy said. "This is a great deal for you."

"Yes, yes, I am interested. *Very* interested."

How could he not be? Coaching, head coaching, was what was missing in his life. It was Darren's drug—the missing link from depression to instant joy.

Darren's doubts eased slightly when Jimmy said, "You don't have to answer to anyone except me. My AD is clear on this—it is you and me. I have a vision, and you are the coach to take us there. We have a chance to turn around one of, if not *the worst*, women's college basketball programs in Division I."

Still uncertain he'd have the university's backing, Darren asked, "Is everyone on board with me becoming the head coach?" The last thing he, or Jimmy for that matter, needed was a battle with the administration.

"Of course. Do you trust me?"

"You are the only one I trust."

"Do we have a deal, Darren?"

"Where do I need to be and when?"

"My people will contact you later today to give you all of the details. I will see you in a few days."

Before he hung up the phone, Darren asked, "Where is this school again? What city?"

"Eagle Gap . . . Eagle Gap, Virginia."

"Oh . . . Ok." Darren needed a map.

BE VISIBLE IN THE COMMUNITY

> *Alone we can do so little; together we can do so much.*
>
> —Helen Keller, Author and Disability Rights Activist

🐾 Jimmy 🐾

The small town of Eagle Gap, Virginia, was just that: small. Its population was exactly 2,242. The residents would tell you it was a sleepy little town. The "I was just resting my eyes" kind of sleepy. With the exception of Jimmy, things moved at two speeds: slow and slower. He thought it was rural America at its best.

The busiest store in town was the Pic & Pac, and Jimmy had quickly become a regular there. The place was an Eagle Gap staple and a true one-stop shop: a post office, coffee shop, deli, and grocery store all in one. If there was a question—or some fresh gossip—the owner, Madie Chisholm, had the answer. The 5'2" fiery, petite senior was a straight shooter whose only bad habits were smok'n and cuss'n. Things were black and white for her—no gray. She was an avid sports fan, ready to quiet the room if the Atlanta Braves were playing, and she was always one of the first in line for a VCSU women's basketball game. Madie had even hung around through their losing seasons; she was loyal to a fault.

A few rolling hills lay outside the city limits of Eagle Gap, home of the Foxhounds—named after Virginia's state dog. Sampson, the live mascot whose baying cheer hyped up the crowds at every home game, held a certain celebrity status in Eagle Gap, even making much-welcomed public appearances on occasion.

VCSU's campus was like its own small city. Every September, the town's population quadrupled as over 7,000 students came to "The Gap." It was a true residential campus, and once a student arrived, they rarely left. If a student did go out of town, Lou from Lou's Filling Station would make sure they left with a full tank of gas and the necessary oil. Lou embodied the spirit of the Eagle Gap residents: friendly to all and ready to go the extra mile for anyone.

When rumors spread about the new women's basketball coach, the quiet town sparked with excitement for a program that was a chronic loser. Everywhere Jimmy went, rumors swirled. No one seemed to know exactly who he was looking to hire—just that it was a former NBA coach in hopes of reviving the struggling women's basketball program. Passionate sports fans knew it could be anyone, too, as the NBA boasts the highest turnover rate among the four most popular professional sports.[2] Jimmy heard Madie's response to the rumors secondhand: "I dunno who Dr. Harding's bring'n in, but they gotta world of hurt staring'um in dare eyes. It'll be like turning a big bass boat 'round inna swimmin pool. But we gonna see, aren't we? I'll be rootin' dem on like always."

Jimmy knew that hiring Darren Blood would be an even more unpopular decision across the women's college basketball landscape than it was in Eagle Gap. The town and students were craving a winner—faculty members and university employees were a little less enthusiastic about the idea of bringing someone like Darren to lead the women's program. In addition to his personal baggage, Darren had never coached women before. The dean of education, Dr. Bernadette Kelly, was not afraid to express her disapproval in an email to Dr. Harding. Jimmy was certain there were others who decided to put their own hot-lettered emails in their drafts, only to never send them. This was an emotional intelligence skill Harding had grasped decades ago from studying Abraham Lincoln, who had mastered the art of regulating his emotions by pouring out his anger in letters but never sending them once he calmed down.[3]*

One thing was for sure: Hiring an unpredictable and volatile coach would place VCSU women's basketball front and center on most sports pages. As some were quietly saying, Harding sure was dumb—dumb like a foxhound. But hiring a controversial coach was intentional and deliberate—two words great leaders and coaches adhere to. Jimmy knew precisely what this hire could do for the university and its women's basketball program. Publicity, good or bad, would grab people's attention.

Within days of hearing the rumors, it became official.

The headline in the local newspaper read, "You Heard Right, Ex-NBA's Blood to Coach Lady Foxhounds." A smile played on his mouth as he read the article. *You better prove me right, Darren,* Jimmy thought. It was on your mark, get set, go. Time to mentor his new coach.

---

* It was a skill Abraham Lincoln used to defuse his anger, writing what he called a "hot letter." He would write the letter but never send it. The most famous letter never sent was addressed to General George Meade, the Union Commander, who failed to possibly end the Civil War by not applying continued pressure on Robert E Lee's army at Gettysburg. The letter, dated July 14, 1863, was never sent.

＊ ＊ ＊

Jimmy Harding was a people person. Darren, not so much. While Jimmy was shaking hands, taking selfies with fans, and striking deals, Darren was a lone wolf, watching game film, studying basketball with a hot coffee close by, and never smiling for photos, let alone seeking them out.

Jimmy's plan was simple: He would mentor his friend and work on those weaknesses. And it began with being visible and accessible. Though his leadership style needed only tweaks, his people skills needed a total rebuild. Darren was a flawed individual. A man with intelligence, yes—temperament, no. He was no FDR.[4] Baggage aside, Darren Blood could teach like few others. He needed this program, and the program needed him. It was up to Harding to see that both became winners. Serial winners.

The Pic & Pac opened for business at 5:30 a.m., the magical hour when the entering bells tinged, the door squeaked, and the wood floors creaked. Delicious smells flooded the store from all directions: fresh coffee, baked goods, and deli meats. The walls were decorated with photos from decades past. The Pic & Pac served as a tribute to a time before, a conduit for the world of today, and a promise of the future of Eagle Gap. For Jimmy, it was where he could find the greatest sparks of creativity.

Experience taught him that getting out to meet people and make friends was essential. You needed to learn about the culture of the town, what made it run, and, more importantly, *who* made it run. The Pic & Pac, Jimmy decided, was his place to do business with his new basketball coach.

The meeting was scheduled for 7:31 a.m.—Jimmy always chose ultra-specific times to help people remember them, a form of exactness. While Darren had seemed confused as to why it was 7:31 and not 7:30, he didn't push back. *A good sign,* thought Jimmy. He arrived 15 minutes early, following the Lombardi Time Principle—if you are not 15 minutes early, you are 15 minutes late. Jimmy always told his people that being on time was critical. It builds trust, dependability, and confidence. He knew that if you are late, you are telling someone your time is more important than theirs, and this can quickly become a bad habit.[5]

Madie welcomed the president with a coffee and said, "So, I hear ya bring'in da coach this morning?"

"Yes, ma'am, I am," he answered with the utmost respect. That was the only way to speak to Madie, and any resident of Eagle Gap was happy to correct someone for using anything less. But Harding wondered, *How the hell does she know this? Ms. Madie still owns a flip phone, and even if she has a computer at home, I'm none too sure she could even turn it on.*

"It's the best place in town, fer sure. Can't get better than here. You'll see," Madie said. "We like havin' ya here too, Mr. President." She paused as she wiped down the table. "The last president? Never saw'em. Didn't seen a head coach either. Notta once. So, this is nice. Rilly rilly nice to see, Dr. Hardin'."

"You can call me Jimmy."

"Ya sure?"

"Yes, I am sure." Madie smiled and walked away. In his own mind, Dr. James Harding had only ever been Jimmy. He was no big deal. Jimmy pulled out his journal and began to write. Journaling was something he started years ago. Years committed to this habit had vastly improved his mental health. Daily journaling helped clear his mind of the negative and focus on the positive. It kept his emotions in check.[6]

Jimmy was still writing when, at 7:28 a.m., Darren Blood walked in. At 5'10", 170 lbs of lean muscle, Darren was still fit enough to play. His body language projected an air of confidence. Jimmy loved that about his former teammate. Even after being beaten down and told he didn't belong on the court ever again, Darren still carried himself with the pride and surety of a coach. He looked exactly how Jimmy wanted him to look: unshakeable and in charge. As he walked toward Jimmy, Darren nodded to the patrons who were sitting and enjoying their coffee. He seemed to have a new lease on his life, and Jimmy supposed he did now. Darren was at a turning point in his career. And like with many successful business turnarounds, a sense of urgency was the first ingredient to make it happen.[7]

PHILOSOPHY STARTS WITH VISION

> *Begin with the end in mind.*
> —Steven Covey, Author and
> Motivational Speaker

🐾 Jimmy 🐾

As he held his freshly brewed coffee (always the same: a dash of 2 percent milk with a packet of raw sugar) in one hand, he used the other to pass Darren a leather-bound journal. "Here is an early present to keep our meeting notes, team notes, and personal notes in. Take it with you everywhere."

"Thank you, Jimmy."

"Are you ready for this journey? Personally, I am *pumped up*, Darren. I have not been this excited since I was coaching." Without taking a breath, Jimmy continued, "This program needs a lot: leadership first and quality coaching second." The urgency was evident.

Darren quickly interjected, "Before you say anything, I want to say I appreciate this opportunity. Don't think for a second I don't. I blew it before. I'm definitely ready now . . . This is a blessing. So, again, thank you. I missed coaching." He chuckled dryly to pass over the vulnerable moment, maintaining his tough-guy persona. "Let's go, I am all in."

Jimmy held back a smile as he got down to business, "Leaders all agree on the need for a vision—a compelling vision, strong enough to get others to follow you. For you, that vision is to become a complete coach. You've got the experience and the skills to coach, but we got to develop that EQ. It makes a difference. A leader cannot get by with just IQ—you need EQ to lead a team. Coaches seem to think it's all about strategy, but you've gotta connect with your people. Relationships are so important."[8]

"I never thought about that," Darren said, "or really know what you mean. What the hell is EQ exactly?"

"Your emotional intelligence. EQ encompasses many things, but for you, it means controlling your emotions, overcoming challenges, and defusing conflict. I've read the research, Darren," Jimmy pushed on as he saw the skeptical look on Darren's face. "Experts conclude that emotional intelligence is the hidden driver of excellence. Know that IQ is only responsible for 20 percent of one's success. Your emotional and social intelligence are much greater determinants of the success you'll achieve in your life.[9] You're the coach, but your job is more than teaching and coaching—you have to create an environment where players and staff can be their best selves and reach their goals. A psychologically safe environment. That's EQ."[10]

Darren surprised Jimmy with a very honest response, "I've never bothered with any of that. But I trust you know your stuff. I wouldn't even be here if it weren't for you, so I'm completely open to any and all of your advice. You tell me to do something, I'll do it."

"That's the first step. I just need you to commit to the process," Jimmy said. "As far as the program goes, the vision is simple: win a championship. You must picture that finish line. See the victory parade down Main Street, then plan the steps to get there—reverse engineer it. Every day and night, visualize the team cutting the nets down.*

It seems silly, but it works—that's how I became university president. Your mind takes a mental picture of that vision and goes to work to make it happen. So, Darren, what are you thinking?"

"My style has always been organized and detailed, but I try to coach as if my players are going to be coaches. I've always believed in putting as much pressure on my players to compete during the toughest moments. Everything we do happens at game speed."

"Love it," Jimmy said, "I always take my vision, define the goals to reach it, add the right people, and construct the ideal environment for the team to best use their skills. Then we do the work . . . *together.*"

"That is a tight philosophy," Darren said, scribbling this down in his new journal.

Jimmy said, "Easy to say, but there's work to do first. We need to improve your people skills. First, though, we need to surround you with the right assistant coaches and players. This isn't pro basketball. You aren't working with men in their 20s and 30s with years spent developing extraordinary skills. We're talking about a group of young women who are used to losing. They have never had a coach like you. And they are not

---

* Jimmy Valvano did a little more than visualize. Once a year, he would have his NC State team practice cutting down the nets, as featured in the ESPN *30 for 30* documentary *Survive and Advance.* NC State won the NCAA National Championship in 1983.

professionals. It's your job to help them excel. This is a litmus test for you—connect with each player. Set the example with your attitude. Have great energy and enthusiasm. Control that temper. It will be an adjustment for everyone, but you need to create a place where these girls want to be."

Darren glanced down briefly and then made eye contact. Jimmy was relieved; he wanted Darren to use direct engagement, even during hard conversations.

Jimmy continued, "Remember, *you* are the culture. As you go, we go. You are the head coach. They will follow your lead. You must set the example each day with your attitude *and* your performance. Be the coach and the mentor these girls need. On a scale of 1 to 10, be a Level 10 coach. I know that's possible for you, Darren."

🏀 Darren 🏀

Darren knew he hadn't been the best version of himself in years, perhaps decades. *Wait a minute,* he thought, *maybe I've **never** been the best version of myself.* He'd had a bit of a temper and struggled with self-control as an athlete; those only compounded with the stress of coaching. Then he added in the drinking and self-isolating, and his problems only got worse. Darren regretted it. *Time to make changes.* Nearing 60 years old, he needed to figure out this EQ part of coaching: how to deal with player mistakes, miscommunication with his staff, his team's execution, his interactions with the media, and even his response to criticism. Thank goodness Jimmy was there with the opportunity and wisdom—Darren was committed to the opportunity.

"Okay, let's summarize this," said Jimmy. "We need to focus on doing the work that winning requires. Get the right people." Darren was impressed by Jimmy's confidence. "Time to create a safe environment that screams excellence. You and the staff will work to carry out our vision. We need to fall in love with the process. Simple but very difficult to do. It'll take time."

Darren agreed, "The Lady Foxhounds have proven winning difficult and losing easy. They have finished last in the conference for seven straight years. Seven! It's a Mount Everest of challenges in our sights."

Jimmy nodded earnestly, "Everything we do will be about winning. If it's not about winning, toss it. Embrace a sense of urgency in all phases. Everything counts. Even the hot chocolate must be hot at the concession stand."

It was sweet music to Darren's ears. He needed Jimmy's full support for such a massive personal transformation, but he felt ready to do his part. That meant hiring a new coaching staff. Darren said goodbye to Jimmy, thanked him for his time, and walked out of Pic & Pac with his mind reeling.

Darren knew his history would deter some applicants. He did, however, have one thing on his side: world-class experience. Difficult as he may be, to work with Darren meant working with someone who had coached some of the best players in the world. As Darren headed toward his car, he focused on his next goal: finding three incredible assistant coaches who would help him pull off the greatest turnaround in women's college basketball history.

5 GREAT COMPANY WINS

🐾 Jimmy 🐾

Jimmy had a simple, powerful philosophy when making a critical hire: Surround yourself with the best people and let them work. He'd done his research and knew that even sitting near successful people can improve performance—a team led by successful staff would be unstoppable.[11] Jimmy repeated his plan of attack: *Eliminate obstacles, empower the people, and let them go to work.*

Jimmy knew that VCSU women's basketball started at a disadvantage. He faced the obstacle of Darren's reputation. He was a micromanager and challenging to work with. Extremely tough on players and even tougher on coaches. When he was fired from the Knicks, his assistant coaches didn't bother to defend him. One former coach said, "After games, we immediately watched the film well into the night, critically grading it with a fine-toothed comb. And if we were on the road, we would return home and go straight to the film room. It was basketball 24/7/365. We never got a break."

Another former assistant said, days after his firing, "He was a ticking time bomb. I'm not surprised at what happened. He knows basketball, but it ends there. There is zero personal connection. I never had a real conversation with him."

Officials at Okaloosa-Walton said little, except, "Blood was not a good fit, so we decided to move away from him."

Jimmy shook his head as he remembered these particularly tough reviews. He knew that together, they were turning the page. Harding was watching the hiring process at a measured distance—after ensuring Darren was clear on the supportive staff they needed: a balanced, diverse team with elite experience, the ability to recruit, individual competence, high character, skill with teaching, a high level of emotional intelligence, as well as personal and professional goals.

Even with Jimmy's experience, he knew Darren had to make the final hiring decisions if he was going to be able to trust them.

In conversation with Darren, Jimmy added another layer of advice. "Hire the best coaches—of course—but let them work. Give up control. Delegate important things, not just the mundane. Remember, you cannot do it all. I don't care if you think you can. Teach them and develop them to be a great head coach someday. Coach the coaches. Ask for their input. People want to know you trust, believe, and value their opinions. This is a big step toward improving your interpersonal skills, awareness, and overall professionalism." Harding had watched as Darren wrote all of this down in his journal.

Jimmy knew he had surprised Darren with his next point. "A lot of these administrators, ADs, and search firms are not as smart as you'd think. They target the shiny object of the moment. One-hit wonders. They chase the untested names even when there's proof this approach does not work. Look at the millions of dead money paid to coaches to not coach at all."[12]

Jimmy continued, "I want people who have been in the trenches. People who have won with less, driven vans, swept the floor, and are owners of a blue-collar, white-belt mentality. Persistent. They understand winning is dirty. These are the types of college coaches who will help us build a sustainable program."

With their priorities in alignment, Jimmy watched as Darren hired coaches he believed would fit the program's new vision. Three of the four had experience as head coaches on the college level, which was crucial, plus experience coaching at different levels. They say experience does not matter until you have it.

Harding saw the staff paperwork come through and was pleasantly surprised to see the names and resumes. Although Blood had severed ties within basketball circles, he still knew enough people to point him in the direction of excellent coaches who fit what he needed. The staff included Sandy Mays, Debbie Bennet, Lauren Morris, and Jackson Alexander. Mays was a top DI assistant coach at George Mason with DIII head coaching experience at Bridgewater College. Bennet was the head coach at DII's Georgia Southwestern, Lauren Morris at Junior College's Rowan College of South Jersey. And Jackson Alexander had just finished his second year as a graduate assistant coach at the nearby University of Virginia, where he had also played for four years. It was a stacked staff.

Now that the staffing hurdle was behind them, Jimmy planned the all-important coaches' retreat. Having experienced several turnarounds in his career, Jimmy knew a retreat was a crucial step, particularly to ensure Darren could align with his team. *A time to unite as a staff, evaluate the athletes, and establish team standards,* Harding thought as he notified Darren of the dates. They also needed to define a plan for the season, from A to Z, while recognizing the need to make the adjustment (MTA) and manage moments to pursue long-term success. It was a lot of information to cover, but Jimmy knew they were up for the challenge. Darren's response dinged a moment later: "Can't wait."

Jimmy recognized the growth Darren was already showing. Once upon a time, Darren would have been too arrogant to embrace the retreat idea; he would have blown it off as unimportant.

WHAT DO YOU THINK?

> *Coming together is a beginning, staying together is progress, and working together is success.*
>
> —Henry Ford, Industrialist and Founder of Ford Motor Co.

✎ Darren ✐

The coaches' retreat was a two-day, coach-only getaway with complete privacy. Jimmy provided an upscale meeting room for the coaches, and four different local restaurants catered breakfast and lunch. The community connection was evident; Jimmy's style was to take care of his people, the community included. Equipped with new laptops and personal journals, Darren and his staff were ready to focus on basketball—no distractions.

Darren was uncomfortably nervous but prepared to face the first day, which was dedicated to time-blocking and scheduling, the program's standards, practice, games, and overall philosophy.

As Darren was about to walk into the room, he received a text message. It read, *"Remember to ask your coaches what they think. Let them offer ideas. Listen. It does not have to be your idea or even the idea you choose—just consider it, and enjoy the first steps of transforming this program."*

At 7:59 a.m. precisely, Darren stood before his newly formed staff. "This is an exciting time for each of us. I have not been a head coach for many years. That means I will be learning from you. Your ideas matter. I haven't always been the best listener . . . a terrible listener actually, but that's going to change. Please do not hesitate to interject. I have always been a bit of a loner, doing everything myself. It got me in trouble. Just be patient with me as I adapt."

Before they began, Darren asked each coach to offer their viewpoints on how to take on the program shift and upcoming season.

Coach Debbie Bennet answered first. "We must focus on strategies that will lead to long-term success. While we may see little results at first, it's essential to prioritize cultural changes."

Coach Sandy Mays added to her point, "These girls only know losing, a defeatist attitude. That's a major obstacle if we can't get their attitudes in check."

Coach Lauren Morris said, "We must stay positive and focus on achieving small wins. Instead of worrying about games, let's work on winning our first practice."

Coach Jackson Alexander finished with, "I know from my experience as a player—which was only two years ago—that we were better when the coaches made us feel important. They set aside time for each of us."

"Thank you. This is very helpful. Some great observations," Darren said. He had never been quick to compliment anyone—especially a coach—but he was giving the whole "open emotion" approach a try.

"For me, my focus has always been to teach the game. Teach, teach, teach. Full speed at every turn. Every drill was important," Darren said. He often thought back to his time coaching at the NBA level. His style of go, go, go had backfired over time. His team had burned out, visibly tired of his demanding, relentless methods. This was the chance to try something different.

Together, the coaches agreed that consistency in all program phases was essential for long-term success. And if they had to, make the adjustment, manage it, and then get back on track. Establishing a routine would be essential. Practices, games, conditioning, travel, and meetings had to align with a consistent routine. The overall structure would be built around improving as individuals and as a team. Communication had to be crystal clear—everyone had to be on the same page.

The coaches moved on to the second key component—the program's standards. Darren had studied the work of many great coaches. He was a big John Madden fan. He respected how the man had straightforward, simple standards, preferring to skip over a multitude of suffocating rules—just like Tim Corbin has done with his Vanderbilt baseball teams.[13] Team standards. A simple expectation of excellence. Together, Darren and his staff identified a foundation that included the following three: be on time, pay attention, and give 100 percent effort at all times. When it came to winning basketball, Darren used a Bob Knight axiom: "You have to get more shots than your opponents do, and you have to get better shots."[14]

Practice and game strategy were Darren's strengths, and he was ready to use those, along with their defined foundation, to strengthen the team. Wrapping up that part of the conversation, Darren asked, "Can we teach within that framework?"

They all agreed. Clear and simple.

The focus would be the fundamentals. Each coach had ideas on what they thought was most important. As the conversation continued, Darren did his best to listen. He bit his tongue. The consensus on defense was to keep it simple. The coaches would stress communication, positioning, and the fundamentals of guarding the ball. Darren knew man-to-man defense best from the NBA—zone, not so much. He knew he'd have to lean on his staff here. For offense, the priority would be creating high-percentage shots. Passing and movement without the ball would be heavily emphasized as well. They then discussed drills, illustrated them, and added the drills to their plan.

As a group, they kept reiterating the need for consistency, simplicity, and clarity. If they respected those, they could maintain their three standards. It was a successful day, but Darren walked away feeling a little unsure—and exhausted. *Is this what it means to be a leader?* Sitting quiet on the sidelines as the other coaches talked didn't make him feel like much of a head coach. But Darren knew he had to trust Jimmy.

🐾 Jimmy 🐾

Jimmy Harding could not wait to see how day one went. Instead of asking Darren, he went to his staff. Intel from the others would make clear how to proceed with Darren. Jimmy used this method frequently in both his coaching and administrative careers. Transparent communication that supported trust-building was often met with good results. Of course, he never talked about another employee. He was a pro's pro.

Sandy Mays told Jimmy, "We accomplished a lot. Darren let us talk. He probably spoke the least of all of us. He even seemed relaxed. Of course, it *is* only the first day. But we got a lot done."

Jimmy was satisfied. Day one was a win, however small.

ATTITUDE DETERMINES YOUR ALTITUDE

> *Talent wins games, but teamwork and intelligence win championships.*
>
> —Michael Jordan, NBA Hall of Fame
> and 6-Time Champion

🎳 Darren 🎳

Day two's focus was the 3–27 record and the roster that contributed to it.

Darren received a text from Jimmy before he joined the other coaches: *"Remember, the bottom line today is the assessment of your players and their development going forward. They've had zero structure and even less coaching. A fresh start is exactly what they need. Enjoy the day."*

Prior to gathering, each coach had taken the time to watch films from the previous season and write down their thoughts. Darren started the discussion by asking, "What do you think about this roster?"

Coach Mays said, "Each player needs to be pushed and held accountable. There's a lot of underdeveloped talent here. We need to push 'em to be better. They've settled for average—it's time to expect more."

Coach Bennet added, "We need to decide what a Lady Foxhound player should look like so they have something to strive for. What are the characteristics? What defines who we are? Our players need to have input on what a Foxhound should be—it'll be our job to hold them accountable."

"That's a great idea," said Darren. "In my extensive experience, the number one factor for recruiting is not talent. Yes, the athletes must be talented. But it's far more important they have a great attitude. My best teams had a collection of great attitudes. If you get someone receptive to learning, someone who listens and is passionate about their goals, we will succeed. And when you gather talented people with outstanding attitudes, you will cultivate that synergy." Darren turned to the coaches. "What do you think?"

Coach Mays added, "I want players with a committed work ethic."

"I want them to be selfless and team-oriented," Coach Bennet said.

Coach Morris chimed in. "Do they love basketball? They can't reach their full potential if they don't."

"Totally agree with that one," Darren responded as he wrote their responses on the whiteboard. "Most people are great at what they love. Coach Alexander, do you have anything to add?"

"There are three traits I look for. Are they competitive? Coachable? Athletic?"

"Excellent choices. We all understand talent is critical. You can lose with talent, but you'll never win without it." Switching gears, Darren asked, "Now that you've watched the film, how many players do we have now that fit these characteristics?"

"Two!" The coaches answered simultaneously.

Coach Alexander made it clear who he thought the best player was: "Patricia Crowe is a star. She jumps off the screen—almost literally. She's quick. She has all of the tools: agility, explosive energy, handles the ball, and is a threat to score from anywhere on the court . . . How'd she end up here? I don't know, but we're damn lucky to have her!"

The coaches unanimously agreed with this. Darren, as a former point guard, had noticed Vivian Peck. "What do you think about Peck?"

"Like her," everyone agreed.

"Now, let's get to the hard conversation. Who will struggle the most with the program changes?"

Coach Morris pointed out what she knew everyone else saw: "Seniors Tiffany Hitchcock and Dominique Slade played uninspired and sometimes looked like they quit while on the court. We may have issues with those two. Potential to be energy vampires and suck all the energy and good attitude out of the team.[15] If you watch them from the last season, their body language went south when the game went badly. Losing creates these bad habits. We've got to change it."

Coach Mays added, "Ruby Davis is athletic, but she is another one who underachieved last year. Her production doesn't match her talent level. That tells me she is a little lazy, another behavior dragging the team down. She could be a prominent player for us though. Girl's got game when she's invested. We have to make her care."

"Not an easy task, but I think we can make the adjustment with her." Coach Alexander was determined.

As the conversation continued, Darren asked, "Can we all agree that, early on, we need extensive structure and strict oversight—paying attention to even the smallest details with these girls? A little more old school?" With a slight grin, Darren continued, "I am good at old school, but it'll be different this time. Not my way or the highway, but the plan we all agree on here. I'll be embracing a piece of Dr. Harding's advice: Scream praise, whisper criticism.[15] I have never been a whisperer, but it's time to start."

As the day passed, the assistant coaches felt more comfortable. When disagreements occurred, they were productive. Darren again felt like he was taking a back seat, giving up the authority of a head coach, which made him uncomfortable. But every time he considered taking charge of the conversation, he could hear Jimmy's voice: "You gain more control by relinquishing it." He was skeptical but willing to try.

Continuing on with their review, the coaches ranked the team from best to worst, considering only physical talent. At the top of the list was Patricia Crowe, followed by Vivian Peck. The next three were underachievers with questionable attitudes: Ruby Davis, Dominique Slade, and Tiffany Hitchcock. There was a distinct talent gap between the top five and the rest of the roster. Nora Okoye, Jayla Thorn, Hailey Broyles, and Kelsey Kurtz were clearly going to be role players. Finding a way to effectively use them would be a challenge. Then there were the three untested freshmen: Alicia Knox and twin sisters, Makala and Tiana Wilson. Like most recruits, they had high school resumes indicating they could contribute, so Darren and the coaches were hopeful the freshman could shake up the team a little.

As the second day wound down, the amount of information they covered started to feel overwhelming. Before Darren could call the conversation to an end and summarize the points, Coach Mays took charge, synthesizing everything they had accomplished during the retreat:

"The vision is simple. We will establish a championship culture based on values. Leadership, high standards, accountability, commitment, competitiveness, collective responsibility, and a growth mindset—we need all of these to drive behaviors that will lead to success. Day to day, everything must and will be intentional. Consistent routines. Communication must be crystal clear, with practices aimed at producing better basketball players and doing simple things at the highest level. No shortcuts or easy outs. As the team evolves, we'll continue to build, knowing success is never final."

Darren was impressed with the rundown and thanked Coach Mays before adding his final thoughts: "Players and coaches will have to be flexible. Make the adjustment—MTA. As coaches, we need to model the expected behavior from day one. I want these principles to become synonymous with the Foxhound way of life for *everyone:* the coaches, the players, and all others connected to the program.

Along with a total shift of our culture, the long-term vision is to become a championship program. In the short term, that means having a great first team meeting, winning the first practice, and continuing to improve daily. If it doesn't involve winning or creating a winning mindset, we trash it. We all know this won't be easy."

The coaches were nodding. Coach Bennet chimed in, "To be great, you must do hard things." Everyone agreed.

Darren thanked his coaches and was relieved to have the retreat over. Still, he was surprised that he enjoyed it—not only that, but those were discussions he needed to have with the staff. *I can't wait to talk to Jimmy. He'll be pleased to hear how much we accomplished.* Darren's coaching mojo was coming back. He had not felt this good in a long time.

🐾 Jimmy 🐾

Like day one, Jimmy followed up with Coach Mays to see how day two went. "We covered quite a bit of information. Coach seemed more comfortable with us today. I even saw some of his excitement shine through. Definitely an intense personality though—focused on winning. It was a productive two days, and we now have a great framework to begin the season with. First team meeting is on Wednesday."

Let's see Darren in action, Jimmy thought.

8   HAVE GREAT MEETINGS

> *None of us is as smart as all of us.*
>
> —Ken Blanchard, Author

🏀 Darren 🏀

Jimmy and Darren met almost daily at the Pic & Pac. Early morning regulars were catching on to their routine. Jimmy made it clear that the best leaders are visible and build trust through that. Darren knew he was facing a mountainous task ahead with this basketball program. Each effort he made was another step in Darren's coaching development. As much as he hated it, Darren knew he had to show everyone that he was not the monster Gene Hack made him out to be. Darren made his way into Pic & Pac, shot a quick smile at Madie, and sat down across from Jimmy.

"So, Darren, how was the retreat?" Jimmy asked.

"Well, we covered a lot. Much more than I thought we would. Structure, routines, and practice philosophy. We decided to keep things simple, clear, and consistent with a few standards to live by. We covered each player, ranking them based on performance last year. The consensus is that Patricia

Crowe is our best player, and we have Ruby Davis, who has a ton of talent but is a tad lazy. Plus two senior starters, Tiffany Hitchcock and Dominique Slade, who have underachieved. Some talented incoming freshmen but a host of average players otherwise."

Jimmy asked, "Can we mold this group?"

"Our first meeting is in two days, so I'll know a little more about us then. But yes, we can improve them."

Darren had always coached with old-school principals. Meetings with his NBA team set meeting records for length and often became completely derailed. A former player told Gene Hack not long after Darren was let go, "The place was in total disarray. We had too many meetings. They were constant. Long and unproductive. A total waste of time."

Succinct meetings that brought positive results were outside Darren's wheelhouse. The two-day retreat was a step in the right direction. Darren was entirely outside of his comfort zone. Working with college athletes was different. *This is not the NBA.* Darren was seeing that more than ever.

Luckily, Jimmy had some wisdom to offer: "Any first meeting is critical to a strong start. You have to set the standards and expectations. Establish the intended culture. As a coach and administrator, I have seen plenty of bad meetings in my day—they're annoying and often create dysfunction. That said, I have a set of guidelines for how to run a successful meeting."

Darren sat with pen and pad ready.

"Don't ever meet just to meet. Meet with a plan in mind. That'll also help keep the meetings short and straightforward. Research says our attention span is less than a goldfish—eight seconds. So I'd keep it at 18 minutes—again, using the crazy number rule."[16]

Darren had doubts. "No chance this first meeting can be that short."

Jimmy nodded, "There are exceptions to the rule. Just don't make a habit of them. And if you know it will be a longer meeting, communicate that. Include a break or some food and drinks, etc. Make the experience enjoyable and show that you respect their time." Jimmy continued, "Be prepared and come with an agenda. Put it on paper and hand it out to everyone. I also suggest you send a reminder to everyone the day before with the location, time, and the meeting's objective. Start on time. When you speak, don't ramble. Be concise. Be clear. Be consistent with your message. A person of average intelligence or better can retain 400 words a minute, so speak quickly with emphasis.[17] All of this will go a long way to building the culture you want. Remember, everything counts. You embody the culture."

Darren wrote quickly as Jimmy spoke. "Give others a chance to speak in the meeting. This may be a challenge for the players. It is critical to get the players out of their comfort zone. Lean on your coaches to help here—they're seasoned. An interactive meeting can reduce any tension or confusion. It will also help increase the attention span. You need input from everyone—promotes teamwork. Empower your coaches and players."

"It was a struggle to sit back at the coaches' retreat. But I'm starting to get the hang of it." Darren knew he was not as equipped as he once thought. He'd never really had a meeting strategy, just points to cover. It was a fixed mindset of leading and wouldn't work anymore. But Darren trusted Jimmy to help turn his approach around. Jimmy agreed and added one more nugget. "Always use crazy times when scheduling anything. People remember it better. If you say 8:00 a.m., people will ask what time we start. 'Around 8?' 'Maybe, I don't know.' So, I don't say 8:00—I say 8:03. This also promotes exactness. When I was coaching, I'd say, 'Bus leaves at 3:21.' Rolling out of the lot at 3:21, I never even took roll. I just said, 'Close the door.' This exactness becomes a subtle motivator. You say what you mean and mean what you say. Our games will start at whatever time plus one minute. It will be hard to forget the time."

"Clever. I will try it," Darren said. He jotted it down in his journal.

As they began to wrap up the meeting, several locals stopped by to introduce themselves to the president and the new coach. Handshakes, smiles, nice-to-meet-yous, happy-to-have-yous, and good-lucks fortified Darren for this coaching challenge. He knew he had his detractors, but this environment made it enjoyable to come to work.

It was one more small step toward rebuilding a program. As Darren finished his coffee and stepped out into the morning, he knew there were many more steps to go.

9

GREAT TEAMS HAVE GREAT LEADERS

A leader is one who knows the way, goes the way, and shows the way.

—John Maxwell, Leadership Expert
and Best-Selling Author

🏀 Darren 🏀

"Coach, the hell you up so damn early for?" Madie asked as Darren walked into the Pic & Pac. At 5:32 a.m., it was still pitch black. Coach Blood was the first customer of the day by a long shot.

"Can't sleep. First team meeting later today. Little wound up," responded Darren.

With the first official practice a few days away, sleep was buried under a long list of priorities. A Pic & Pac coffee and scone was his chosen tonic to soothe the nerves.

"Oh hell, you'll be fine," Madie fired back. "We're all excited round here to see whatcha can do wit dem girls. Need a good coach and a swift kick in the ass. Lived 'ere all my life. Doc says yer de coach who can do it. So, let's go."

Darren grinned.

"Just do yer thing. We gotcher back."

Darren was happy he had an ally in Madie. The reassurance helped more than she realized.

Darren drove to The Lewis and parked in his newly personalized parking space. Knowing someone had gone out of their way to mark it for him made him feel important. Darren's heart warmed. It was a small yet meaningful gesture from Jimmy. He later noticed there was no personalized spot for the president. This exemplified the "leaders-eat-last" mentality that Jimmy Harding lived by.[18]

As Darren quietly eased into the arena, only the basketball court's center jump circle was visible, lit by the dusk-to-dawn ceiling light. The court was soon to become Darren's classroom. The sound of a basketball game, bouncing balls, the swish of the nets, and the screeching sneakers were all music to his ears. As he walked onto the empty court, his nerves momentarily vanished. For the first time in a long time, he was happy—and grateful. As Darren continued to walk the perimeter of the court, he stopped. He visualized the crowd, the cheering, the players moving with cat-like quickness, out-maneuvering the opponent. He could see himself standing on the sidelines, instructing his team with energy and enthusiasm.

Darren sat in the seats above the pull-out bleachers. He wanted to relax and take it all in. Within seconds of sitting, he heard voices from the opposite side of the court. *Who in the world is here this early?* he thought. Two young women in basketball gear appeared, carrying gym bags and wheeling a rack of basketballs. Patricia Crowe and Vivian Peck. *Of course.* Darren smiled, pleased with their dedication.

Darren watched and listened, motionless, as these two athletes began to work. Neither had a clue that their new head coach was less than 100 feet away.

Neither one said much. Crowe grabbed a ball, tossed it to Peck, and then grabbed one herself. They each spent 10 minutes working through a dribbling sequence drill right out of the Morgan Wootten playbook.[19] Cross-overs, between the legs, behind the back, and spin moves using both hands. As they both picked up the pace, Crowe barked, "C'MON! Quicker. Faster. Let's go."

Peck accelerated. They followed with two ball drills. Crossovers, a change of cadence with the basketballs, and shifting their pace as they moved forward, backward, and side to side. Two more ball drills took another 10 minutes. They followed with passing drills, then an array of shooting drills from all areas on the court with pressure from the other. They ran a motion offense with two, cutting and screening without taking a shot. "Thatta girl," said Peck when Crowe pushed back with intensity.

They fist-pumped at the end of every drill. Whether they knew it or not, they were improving performance by that basic contact.[20] Darren was even more impressed to see this.

The two walked over to grab their water bottles and towels. Wiping her face, Crowe said, "Let's finish up with our foul shots after we run."

They ran a set of 16s in under a minute. Then, Darren watched them shoot foul shots as their bodies neared exhaustion. He thought, *These two have the idea.* Darren was excited and pleased to see such a strong work ethic. They looked like they enjoyed the grind, the sweat, and some of the pain required to master the skills. As they walked out, they high-fived and started chatting strategy for the season. It was a good sign. These two seemed like the right fit for Darren's philosophy.

Darren was glad to have caught a glimpse of his top players before the staff meeting at 11:11 a.m. They needed to review the meeting agenda to tighten any loose ends. The player meeting was set for 3:31 p.m. Darren could hardly wait.

"This meeting is your tone-setter. Don't talk about basketball or winning. Focus on the values, standards, and expectations. Build on your championship culture today." Darren saw the text from Jimmy flash across his screen and quickly ran through his agenda, waiting to meet the team for the first time.

As the players quietly entered the meeting room, each was given a meeting agenda and mascot-emblazoned notebook. The notebook was the first sign something was different. Coach Bennet was immediately on board with the journal idea when Darren shared his experience with Jimmy. "I love it," Coach Bennet said, "Simple and brilliant. If they write it down, they have a chance to remember it. Plus, it is a good habit."[21] He was enthusiastic.

Crowe opened her notebook, and her expectant gaze made Darren's nervousness rise up—invisible but real. His hands were clammy, and his forehead was glazed with sweat. It was his first time in front of a team as a head coach in over a decade, but Darren did his best to hide his stress.

At 3:31 p.m., Darren promptly introduced himself. His staff followed. Each player was then asked to stand and introduce themselves, say their academic year, tell where they were from, and share their major. Once everyone spoke, Darren had each person go again, and this time, add one thing no one knew about them. This second round was more comfortable. It brought a few smiles and laughs. It was a strategy Coach Morris had used with her teams. Some were hesitant, others not so much. The coaches felt it important for the players to speak in front of their teammates. It would establish a safe environment of camaraderie. The exercise relaxed Darren too—an easy icebreaker to ease them into the real talk.

Darren, against Jimmy's advice, began the meeting with a short, three-minute video: a highlight reel of national women's basketball teams that had won championships—the great UConn and Tennessee teams, followed by South Carolina and LSU. Last-second baskets, great defensive plays, players diving for loose balls, fastbreaks, great passing, toughness, and finally, teams cutting down the nets and hoisting the trophy. As the video faded to black, Darren said, "This is what winning looks like. What you don't see is all the work these teams have done to reach this level. That is the work we will need to do."

Darren continued, "You have to see yourself taking the shot, making the pass, playing smothering defense . . . and then you have to see yourself and your teammates cutting down the nets."

It was not an exercise in imagination. Rather, it was about visualizing the win, manifesting it. That would soon become a staple in their mental preparation.

Darren reinforced the lesson: "I visualized winning every day as an NBA coach. Every day. Make it a habit. Picture winning. This is a habit of excellence." Darren settled in.

"This basketball program is bigger than all of us. But this is *your* program. Just remember how fortunate you are to be here. The opportunity you have been provided. Bear in mind, you don't have to be at this meeting—you get to. Same with practice—you *get* to practice. You don't have to practice. You have a tremendous opportunity to do great things." Darren paused for effect as he turned toward the whiteboard. "Every decision you make from this day forward affects VCSU basketball. If each one of you chooses to work hard, be a great teammate, and do everything you can to improve to help the team, we will be successful. Do hard things. Push and challenge yourself to improve daily—we will be successful."

Darren continued, "Ladies, we're to embrace three standards. Notice I said standards, not rules. The great Tim Corbin always says, 'Rules are for those who cannot follow directions—standards are for those who want to do great things.' We're here to be great.

- ⮕ Let's start by being on time. Get in the habit of being early and staying late.
- ⮕ Pay attention. The coming weeks will be centered around basketball instruction. We have excellent coaches who can teach. Be a sponge.
- ⮕ And when we tell you to go 100 percent, go 100 percent. Being a champion requires maximum effort. Push yourself on the court, whether it's games or 'just' practice. Take that same energy to the weight room. Learn to max out."[22]

Darren knew he had to promote athlete engagement, so he asked someone to repeat the three standards. To no surprise, Crowe's hand shot up with unbridled enthusiasm, "Be on time, pay attention, and go full speed when we're told to."

The silence in the room was deafening. There'd never been standards at VCSU before—not ones they seriously followed. Darren knew this wouldn't be the last discussion of their standards—it was merely the tipoff. Jimmy always preached that repetition is the mother of learning—based on the idea that after a 10-minute chalk talk, a player will lose 50 percent of what was said within 48 hours and only retain 25 percent. Therefore, repetition is key.[23] Preparation would separate the Lady Foxhounds from the rest of the DI pack.

That first meeting was just the start, but he felt things had gone well. Classroom stuff was not necessarily in his wheelhouse; he was excited to get on the court and truly kick off the season. The hardwood was where the sweat, physical pain, and heart-pounding effort took place. Darren's blood started to warm.

WHAT IS A LADY FOXHOUND?

10

> *Show up on time. Know your lines. Have an idea of what to do in the scene. The rest will take care of itself.*
>
> —Paraphrased from Tom Hanks,
> Actor and Film Director

🐾 Darren 🐾

It was unheard of to have a Saturday meeting at 9:07 a.m. before the season even started. The objective was to bring the team together to build their vision of what an elite Lady Foxhound basketball player should be. Darren and the coaches knew that defining the identity of the Lady Foxhounds was vital for a championship culture. With only 14 wins over the last three years, the VCSU Lady Foxhounds needed hope. They needed passion.

Since this meeting would take longer than the introductory one, Darren, inspired by Jimmy catering their coach's retreat, provided breakfast for the team and staff. As he organized the food, Darren repeated Jimmy's most recent bit of advice: "Get input from everyone. The retreat was for the coaches—this meeting is about the players. Every player must have a say in this discussion. Grant them ownership of the program."

As the ladies settled down with full plates, Darren reminded them of the importance of the meeting: "Everyone must understand this is a major step in improving our program. Lock in, pay attention, and speak up."

With a nod to Coach Mays, Darren handed her the floor.

"Welcome to a team-building workshop. Our goal is simple: Determine who the Lady Foxhounds are. Every great team has an identity. Let's define who we are and what we want to look like. Using the index cards in your notebooks, write as many characteristics as possible for a Lady Foxhound player. There are no wrong answers. You have five minutes."

A few ladies hesitated, glancing around at their teammates. In contrast, Crowe and Peck were already filling out the cards, quickly running out of space to write anything else. Eventually, every player had a pencil in hand and was scratching down notes.

When the time was up, Coach Mays asked Coach Morris to take notes on the whiteboard. "Who wants to go first?" asked Coach Morris.

Unsurprisingly, Crowe raised her hand. Dominique and Tiffany rolled their eyes as if to say, "This girl is too much."

Crowe did not seem to notice—but Darren did, and he filed it away for later. Crowe was ready with her top five: "Committed, unselfish, disciplined, respectful, and a great teammate."

The staff looked impressed, but Darren knew they weren't surprised. Early discussions between the coaches had defined Crowe as the hub of the team. As the players took turns sharing their ideas, Coach Morris kept adding to the board until it was filled with nearly 100 words: hustler, relentless, supportive, positive, honest, present, dedicated, leader, coachable, flexible, risk-taker, open to new ideas, accountable, and serving. Darren was thrilled with the participation, though he and the other coaches seemed to notice that Dominique and Tiffany gave lukewarm effort, sharing with only minimal enthusiasm. The most interesting word came from a most unlikely player: junior forward Ruby Davis. Ruby, a physically talented player who had been labeled lazy, gave a simple description: "Be a winner."

That response made Darren take a second look at the 6'3" talent-soaked Ruby Davis. He remembered Coach May and the staff saying at the coaches' retreat, "We need to get Ruby going. Her with Crowe and Peck . . . you may have something to work with."

With every inch now crammed with all the characteristics of a Foxhound, the team needed to synthesize it down to three or so core traits. Mays called attention to this next task, "We need three to five to truly define the Lady Foxhound player. And when any one of us steps outside of these core beliefs, it will be the job of the coaches and their teammates to bring us back in line with our standards."

The team fell silent. Whether they were unsure of which words to choose or thinking through their options, Darren wasn't sure. He chimed in, "There are no wrong answers or bad ideas. No judgment."

Patricia Crowe had little time for any BS and raised her hand. "Grit, to me, is what we all should be about. Relentless effort, hard work, toughness, having a never-quit attitude, persistence. Grit embodies all of these."

Darren nodded. Grit went on the board without any objections.

The discussion continued. Led by the players, they eventually narrowed the identity of a Foxhound player to three core principles: commitment, grit, and excellence. The players believed they should all be committed to the process, possess grit, and seek excellence on and off the court.

As the meeting came to a close, Darren walked to the front of the group. "So, now we have three words to describe a Lady Foxhound. I love what you've decided on together. That leads me to my next point: How do you want me and the other coaches to respond when someone's behavior is not aligned with these three principles? It won't always be easy. You can't just embody the traits when you feel good. You have to work hard, even when you don't feel like it. My best players in the NBA gave 100 percent even when they were tired and sore."

Vivian Peck raised her hand. "Be honest with us. I know sometimes I get down on myself and let a possession go. Just tell me when I'm not playing at the expected standard. "

Junior Jayla Thorn raised her hand.

"Yes, Jayla," said Darren.

"I have been here for two years, and we don't play well when we are constantly told we suck. Or worse, the 'Why are you even here?' comment. For two years, that's basically all we got from Coach. It was negative, negative, negative," she said.

Darren had to pause for a moment. *I have always told the truth and have even said things like that, but my approach must change. I'll need to curb the "Get your head out of your ass, what the hell was that, you're sucking today" type of berating.* It was exactly what Jimmy was telling him. Control your emotions. "I won't be like that," Darren finally said. "The coaches and I will do our best to offer specific, constructive feedback. Can't promise I won't get caught up in the heat of the moment, but I can promise to be respectful. You work hard to embody the Lady Foxhound identity, and I'll work hard to be an example for you."

With a nod of agreement, Coach Mays moved on to review everything they'd discussed: commitment, grit, and excellence as the foundation of a Lady Foxhound player. They could do this by being on time, paying attention, and giving 100 percent. All of this combined would support the program's championship culture. Of course, it would be a process of daily improvement. Small increments. But Darren knew they were up for the challenge.

11 CAMPUS CONNECTIONS

> *If you have the courage to start, you have the courage to succeed.*
>
> —Mel Robbins, Author and
> Self-Help Coach

✎ Darren ✎

Darren was feeling antsy as 9:01 a.m. ticked closer. He wasn't used to being front and center in this type of educational setting, but in an earlier meeting with Jimmy, he had stressed, "The people on this campus need to see your face up close. Get out. Be visible. Be accessible. Sitting at your desk or in the film room doesn't make connections. People skills, Darren, people skills." Jimmy interlocked his finger. "It is all about connecting . . . connecting."

The spacious tan and white conference room with black accents, called the Foxhound Room as an additional gesture of school pride, was decorated with photos of the historic campus and incredible shots of the school's athletic programs. It was motivating. The fact that the meeting occurred in the presidential meeting room sent a small message that the president was serious about rebuilding and sustaining the program. Darren could see Jimmy's influence all around the campus: subtle reminders of the school's and students' accomplishments—a visible effort to encourage Foxhound pride.

The meeting included anyone and everyone connected to the basketball program: university deans, department heads, academic counseling, housing, admissions, financial aid, advancement, dining, facilities, security, campus maintenance, and the new athletic director, Charlie Owens. All the people who could make VCSU better were there. Darren and Charlie Owens had already met and established a relationship, but Darren was grateful that Jimmy had decided to work directly with women's basketball while Owens focused his efforts elsewhere. This was an unorthodox structure, but women's basketball was more important now than ever.

Even with all his preparation, Darren was more than a little uncomfortable with this gathering. VCSU gear was laid out for those in attendance. There were hats, T-shirts, hoodies, key chains, stuffed foxhounds—you name it. All free to grab, go, and market the new brand.

Jimmy had told Darren, "Invite all of these people to our practices. Get as many people involved as possible. Make those connections, Darren." Jimmy was relentless in making his point.

Darren's assistant coaches knew the significance of the campus connection. "Trust me, Coach, if we show everyone we are here to develop our players, run a value-based program, and stress high-level performance, we will grow an on-campus fan base, gain trust, and move a little closer to our vision," Coach Mays said. "It'll take time."

After taking a deep breath, Darren moved to the podium. He began by thanking everyone for attending and acknowledging that women's college basketball was different from what he was used to. "Thankfully, I have the best mentor in the state to help this transition," Darren gestured to Dr. Harding.

Then, Darren introduced his staff and offered his cell number and office hours for anyone who wanted to chat— "even if it's not about the program. I'm always down for a coffee at Pic & Pac." Everyone laughed.

Feeling a little more confident, Darren and his staff shared their vision, values, and plans. They then discussed ways to improve communication and collaboration between the basketball staff and other university departments. Darren took a beat to ask for feedback on enhancing communication between the basketball staff and university leaders. Despite his initial misgivings, the meeting was running similarly to the coaches' retreat.

As they wrapped up, the dean of education, Dr. Bernadette Kelly, stood. "I have a question." Everyone who knew Dr. Kelly knew that she was not in favor of hiring Coach Blood. "I am a fan of college athletics. Always cheering our student-athletes from the sidelines. And I believe in our new president's vision." She turned toward Dr. Harding, giving him a respectful nod. Then, she looked at Darren. "But with your background . . . I know enough to know that many here at the university, including me, do not think you deserve this job. Maybe an NBA job, I can't say—but as a college coach, you're an automatic role model for our students. You've never coached women, and I'm not sure you deserve that honor. So why are you here? Why does Dr. Harding believe you're the right man for the job?" She sat. Jimmy had told Darren that Dr. Kelly was a skeptic, and he knew he could get her on his side. He was confident. But it would take some work.

As tensions in the room escalated, Darren cleared his voice and prepared to respond. He knew there would be other detractors like Dr. Kelly, even if they didn't directly challenge him. His verbal battles with Gene Hack had unknowingly primed him for this negative, sticky situation.

"I am glad you asked, and I appreciate your straightforward approach. Dr. Harding owes me nothing, but he still chose to give me a chance. For that, I owe him. He brought me to VCSU to help revive a program that has not had a winning season in nearly two decades. With women's basketball gaining national interest, it is important for the university to become relevant. I can do that. Coaching women? Coaching is coaching, but I need to learn how to become a better coach and person. To learn how to connect with people. My people skills have always been a weakness. I can coach Dr. Kelly. My record proves it. But I still have a lot to learn. You're welcome to attend and watch our practices any time, as all of you are."

With that, the room visibly deflated. Dr. Kelly seemed satisfied with the answer. Darren shot a look at Jimmy and saw how proud his president and friend was.

The room's noise level rose as everyone filed out. Most everyone grabbed some gear, but Dr. Kelly passed on the gear and exited alone. Darren leaned over to his assistant coaches, "Not a total transformation, but this was a small win for VCSU women's basketball. Nice work, everyone."[24]

12 COMMUNITY SUPPORT

> *The only way to do great work is to love what you do.*
>
> —Steve Jobs, Inventor and
> Co-Founder of Apple Inc.

🎣 Darren 🎣

There were 42 days before VCSU's first game. The number flashed in Darren's mind when he awoke. Today was the first practice. He fretted. "Not enough time. Definitely not," he said to himself. He had yet to master patience. There were challenges in every direction.

Darren strolled into the Pic & Pac 15 minutes earlier than usual to grab a large coffee to go. He spotted a small group of men sitting together, sipping their coffees. Darren could sense something was amiss when they quieted as he walked closer. "Hello, gentlemen," Darren said. He did not know the men by name but recognized them as regulars. Locals had turned it into a ritual to eavesdrop on Coach Blood and Dr. Harding.

"Hey, Coach, how are you this fine morning?" one man asked as he stood up and offered his hand. "Frankie Cornell's the name." They shook hands.

Frankie Allen Cornell was born and raised just down the road in Crozet. He played college basketball at a small nearby college in the mid-1960s. With the ugly shadow of Jim Crow still lurking over the South, it was a tough time for a black youngster to play anywhere. Still, Frankie persisted, and he'd retired and moved back to the area to escape the comings and goings of Hoboken, New Jersey. Frankie was a Knicks season ticket holder and had witnessed Darren attacking the referee that fateful night.

"Coach, did you see the article?" asked Frankie. Darren knew exactly what Frankie was talking about. The *Eagle Gap Gazette* was the local paper. It had picked up *Washington Insider* Gene Hack's article from the day before.

The one-sided article titled "Blood's Last Stand: When a Naive 'Know-It-All' Hires the Desperate" was a personal attack on Darren's character. Hack questioned why VCSU would hire a man whose past was an accurate indication of the person he is—a coach with obvious emotional issues who carries a history of uncontrollable behaviors on the court.

"Oh, yeah, he knows basketball—but little else," the article read. "And it's his poor people skills that trump any ability Blood has as a coach. A low-caliber guy. Dr. Harding and VCSU have some explaining to do."

Hack also took a swing at the impeccable Harding, going deep into their friendship that began in high school. "The good ole boys' system," Gene claimed. "In the end, Harding will look even more foolish than he does now. Blood can coach, but there will be a price to pay. Stay tuned."

The article's timing was Hack's way of causing a stir in a town where the slightest conflict mirrored the Cuban Missile Crisis.

"Hello, all," Darren Blood offered his hand to each. Frankie stepped forward to introduce himself and the others. "This is Pauly Fulton, Sonny Lamp, Robby Stokes, and Willie Langloh. We call ourselves the Foxhound Phanatics. We go to every game no matter how bad things get." All five were retired and enjoyed the quiet serenity of Eagle Gap, Virginia, where slow was just fast enough. They all had a passion for basketball.

Frankie added, "Was a Knicks season ticket holder for years . . . worked across the Hudson for 30 years as a police officer. Yep, New Jersey . . . the Shore, Springsteen, Ice-T, Nicholson, Sinatra . . . the whole bit . . . It is a pretty cool place . . . great pizza . . . anyhow."

"So, you know?" asked Darren. "About my past?"

"Don't matter," said Frankie, as he waved it off with his hand. "Shit happens."

"Whatcha think, Coach? Can you turn this thing around?" asked Pauly.

Before Darren could answer, Willie said, "They struggle. Got talent, but it just vanishes—fast too." The article was old news already.

"That Crowe. She's gonna be good," added Sonny.

"Yeah . . . definitely," said Willie. Everyone was nodding with approval.

Unbeknownst to Darren, Jimmy had made friends with the aptly named Foxhound Phanatics, making it a little easier for the new coach to transition to Eagle Gap and VCSU.

"We like Peck and Crowe," Darren said. "They have something we can build on."

"Y'all like Peck too? I can see it. Yes sir, absolutely," added Willie. "Tough. Grinder."

Sonny piped in with a suggestion. "Can we come to practice one day to watch?"

"I don't see why not," Darren said. "We've offered it to everyone else. No rule says you can't."

Frankie said, "Coach, between you, me, and the boys, we are glad to have you. We know you can do it. Doc Harding thinks high of you, and he told us not to believe everything we read about you. He said you can coach, so by golly, we're with you."

Darren genuinely appreciated this group of men. He felt their sincerity. He could not remember the last time he felt this way.

"It was a pleasure meeting you. Have a great rest of the day. And Sonny, I'll check on that practice thing." Darren turned to head back to where the busy Madie was tending to customers.

"So, you finally got to meet dem Foxhound Phanatics," Madie said. "Good guys, they are. The usual?"

Darren thought he never had a relationship with any fan, much less five of them whose combined age was over 300. As Darren walked out to head to his car, his cell buzzed, "*Saw the article. You cannot control what you cannot control. Have a great first practice. Go Hounds!—Jimmy.*"

Emotionally, Coach Blood was in a better place where he felt appreciated. He didn't realize how much it meant to be lifted up by others: five strangers he'd just met, the reliable old Madie, and a friend he'd known his entire life. And he was hours away from doing what he loved most: coaching basketball. For the first time in a while, he felt good.

SUMMARY OF PART I:
BUILDING THE FOUNDATION

1. **Hire for Emotional Intelligence**

   Emotional intelligence is key to effective leadership. High EQ leaders are good listeners, delegate well, and value their teams. They clearly communicate, inspire loyalty, and efficiently handle conflicts. In times of pressure, these leaders stay calm, helping their teams focus, reduce anxiety, and enhance productivity.

2. **Develop a Compelling Vision and Take Action**

   Vision is the cornerstone of leadership. Without it, individuals and teams can lose direction, focus, and motivation. Leaders must also be action-oriented. Vision alone doesn't lead to success, unless it's followed by an actionable plan.

3. **Surround Yourself with a Strong Team and Let Them Work**

   "Giving up control to gain control" is an important mindset that many leaders find hard to accept. By delegating tasks and trusting others, you can build confidence and encourage creativity within your team. People perform better when they feel trusted and valued. Create that psychologically safe environment.

4. **Prioritize Visibility and Presence**

   By getting out of the office and connecting with your people, you can build a rapport with your team and your supporters. It is an important element of leadership.

5. **Establish a Championship Culture**

   The first meeting is the key moment for setting expectations, standards, and the intended culture. Culture drives behavior that gets results. As a leader, you set the tone, and your actions early on will influence how that culture evolves.

6. **Build Trust**

   Sometimes it's as simple as listening and asking, "What do you think?" Done right, the question can be an incredibly impactful way to empower others and build trust. Leaders who listen and seek input demonstrate that they value others' ideas. This creates a sense of ownership and mutual respect.

7. **Take Risks and Encourage Creativity**

   To lead, you must take risks. Making bold decisions often separates successful leaders from unsuccessful leaders. Take calculated risks. Always encourage creative thinking. Thinking outside the box drives innovation and progress, separating your team or organization from the pack.

8. **Ask Yourself, Does This Choice Improve the Organization?**

   When deciding on what to do to improve results, ask yourself, is what we are about to do going to make us better? The team better? The organization better? If the answer is no, move away. If the answer is yes, implement it. The British Rowing Team enacted this philosophy as they prepared for the Olympics, always asking, "What will make the boat go faster?" They only took action if it got them closer to winning.[25]

PART I
REFERENCES

1. Matt McGowan, "Caitlin Clark and Iowa Fans Drive Demand, Prices for Final Four Tickets," *USA Today*, April 3, 2024, https://www.usatoday.com/story/sports/ncaaw/2024/04/03/womens-final-four-caitlin-clark-iowa-fans-tickets/73193712007/.

2. "Comparing Coach Turnovers in the NBA, NHL, NFL, and MLB," OnlineGambling.ca, accessed February 20, 2024, https://www.onlinegambling.ca/content-hub/comparing-coach-turnovers.php.

3. Doris Kearns Goodwin, *Leadership: In Turbulent Times* (Simon & Schuster, 2018).

4. Doris Kearns Goodwin, *Teaches U.S. Presidential History and Leadership,* MasterClass, accessed September 11, 2024, video, https://www.masterclass.com/classes/doris-kearns-goodwin-teaches-us-presidential-history-and-leadership.

5. David Maraniss, *When Pride Still Mattered: A Life of Vince Lombardi* (Simon & Shuster, 2000).

6. Julia Cameron, *The Artist's Way: A Spiritual Path to Higher Creativity* (TarcherPerigee, 2022).

7. John P. Kotter, *Leading Change* (Harvard Business Press, 1996).

8. Daniel Goleman, *Emotional Intelligence: Why It Can Matter More Than IQ* (Bloomsbury, 1996).

9. John Chancellor, "Why Emotional Intelligence (EQ) Is More Important Than IQ," Owlcation, January 22, 2024, https://owlcation.com/social-sciences/Why-Emotional-Intelligence-is-More-Important-Than-IQ.

10. Jonathan T. Chan and Clifford J. Mallet, "The Value of Emotional Intelligence for High Performance Coaching," *International Journal of Sports Science & Coaching* 6, no. 3 (2011): 315–328, https://doi.org/10.1260/1747-9541.6.3.315.

11. Emily Stone, "Sitting Near a High-Performer Can Make You Better at Your Job," Kellogg Insight, May 8, 2017, https://insight.kellogg.northwestern.edu/article/sitting-near-a-high-performer-can-make-you-better-at-your-job.

12. Paula LaVigne, "$146M in Buyouts Owed to Fired Power 5 Football Coaches Since '22," ABC News, November 14, 2023, https://abcnews.go.com/Sports/146m-buyouts-owed-fired-power-5-footballcoaches/story?id=104874479#:~:text=According%20to%20an%20ESPN%20analysis,31%2C%20202.

13. Barry Davis, "Transformation, Leadership, Culture: A Qualitative Study on Elite NCAA Head Baseball Coaches" (PhD diss., Concordia University of Chicago, 2019).

14. "Bob Knight - Clinic 1: An Approach to Teaching (1983)," posted April 2, 2018, YouTube, 6 min., 10 sec., https://www.youtube.com/watch?v=QCEUXE3Cjag.

15. Jon Gordon, *The Power of Positive Leadership: How and Why Positive Leaders Transform Teams and Organizations and Change the World* (John Wiley & Sons, 2017).

16. K. R. Subramanian, "Myth and Mystery of Shrinking Attention Span," *International Journal of Trend in Research and Development* 5, no. 3 (2018): https://www.ijtrd.com/papers/ijtrd16531.pdf.

17. "Tony Mason - Coaching Clinic," posted June 7, 2017, YouTube, 1 hr., 22 min., 34 sec., https://www.youtube.com/watch?v=Pl64iVMCVAU.

18. Simon Sinek, *Leaders Eat Last: Why Some Teams Pull Together and Others Don't* (Penguin Random House, 2014).

19. Morgan Wootten and Joe Wootten, *Coaching Basketball Successfully* (Human Kinetics, 2013).

20. Dacher Keltner, "Positive Contact Between Teammates Related to Better Athletic Performance," from Positive Coaching Alliance, posted March 16, 2017, YouTube, 1 min., 32 sec., https://devzone.positivecoach.org/resource/video/positive-contact-between-teammates-related-better-athletic-performance.

21. Andrew O'Toole, *Paul Brown: The Rise and Fall and Rise Again of Football's Most Innovative Coach*, (Clerisy Press, 2008).

22. "John Madden: A Name Synonymous with Football | A Football Life," posted January 4, 2022, YouTube, 43 min., 7 sec., https://www.youtube.com/watch?v=Zc75Vrahc3M&list=PL1SLMQpQrlizn6u4LLZeRhiZBD4Zl6_1o&index=1.

23. "Tony Mason - Coaching Clinic," posted June 7, 2017, YouTube, 1 hr., 22 min., 34 sec., https://www.youtube.com/watch?v=Pl64iVMCVAU.

24. John P. Kotter, *Leading Change* (Harvard Business School Press, 1996).

25. Benjamin Hardy, "This One Question Will Make Every Decision in Your Life Easier," Medium, March 1, 2018, https://medium.com/@benjaminhardy/this-1-powerful-strategy-made-the-british-rowing-team-to-go-from-average-to-winning-olympic-gold-b859b7f6cda1.

PART II
PREPARATION

SET THE EXAMPLE

> *You have to work hard in the dark to shine in the light.*
>
> —Kobe Bryant, NBA Hall of Fame and 5-Time Champion

⚒ Darren ⚒

Darren's stomach was uneasy, a nervous emptiness as he exited his office and walked toward the meeting room. It had been a while. As he pulled the door open to enter, he reminded himself, *Be the leader. The best head coach in America. Set the example. Set the tone.*

Running a practice was Darren's happy place. Here, he was a championship coach. It was where his confidence soared. As Darren took his place in front of the team, who were locked in to hear what this former NBA coach had to say, he began, "Practice is critical to success. But first, we must learn *how* to practice. Value practice and the effort it requires. It is where becoming a champion begins. You must be willing to do the work and then the extra work before and after to develop championship habits."

Every player was paying close attention except Tiffany Hitchcock. Darren did a double-take; Tiffany was not even in the room.

Each player was given an agenda sheet. It read: "Work the Process," followed by the keywords "Effort. Consistency. Simplicity. Execution." The sheet also displayed a practice routine the team would follow daily. The assistant coaches were given the task of producing the daily agenda after their daily coaches' meetings.

Darren continued, "The practice philosophy is to simplify and execute. We'll be moving at game speed, ladies, unless we say different. I need effort—can't stress it enough. Execute the fundamentals: ball movement, cutting, screening, getting good shots, rebounding, defending the entire 94 feet. We'll embrace routine and repetition to perform at the highest level. Everything we do will be deliberate—no wasted drills." He paused. "Let me say this again—everything we do in practice will be at game speed. Practice will be tougher than any game we play. It will require mental quickness as we will rotate drills without delay. You must learn to react instinctively. All practices will end with a short Well-Better-How discussion." He surveyed the room, then asked, "What questions do you have for me?" No one raised a hand. They were slightly intimidated by his presence. Darren was settling in, but he was still finding his way.

Jimmy had told him to make the plan crystal clear—no confusion about the approach to the season.

At 3:06 p.m., Darren instructed the team to put away their journals and get ready to practice. He refused to call attention to Tiffany, who had finally bothered to join them. The staff made their way to the court ahead of the team. A flurry of basketballs bounced toward the team as they followed the coaches. "Thank you, Jess," said Peck and Crowe in unison. Peck and Crowe were the first to emerge from the meeting room. Jess was one of the six student managers employed by the VCSU coaching staff. Jess had been loyal to the Lady Foxhounds since her freshman year, and more than anything, she wanted to become a college head coach one day. Darren had never had student managers, but he discovered quickly she was going to be an asset. After all, managers are one of the most important components of any successful athletic program and often go on to gain other positions within an organization. Some even became high-level head basketball coaches.[1, 2]

Before they started their pre-practice routine, Darren noticed one thing. Except for Crowe and Peck, every other player walked onto the court. There was about a 30-foot walkway from the auditorium entrance to the corner of the court. Plenty of room to run onto the court. In the previous three weeks of player-led workouts, which were mostly pick-up games, the players arrived on their own time, policing themselves. The coaches had hoped the players would develop leadership within the group—a deliberate coaching technique. It was a noticeable swing and a miss.

The visible lack of energy, plus Tiffany's tardiness, triggered Darren's emotional state. His energy was already high with excitement for the practice, but it was now coupled with annoyance. Knee-jerk reactions in the past had resulted in lengthy lectures and obscenities or the entire team running touch-and-goes the length of the court while wearing 25-pound vests. But this time, Darren said nothing. Coach Mays blew the whistle and shifted from pre-practice warm-up to drills.

One particular tactic Darren employed was adding pressure to any drill. Most notably on defense, where they would often scrimmage five-on-four half-court instead of the customary five-on-five full-court scrimmage. All rotations were from offense to defense to out in specific drills, forcing the defender to work while being more fatigued. Pressure was a key principle in every practice. Especially a shooting drill. "A shooting drill without pressure is the biggest waste of time. It's not realistic preparation for a game." Practice must resemble game situations.

Over the two hours, the coaches led varied drills that changed but maintained the structure and the concepts. They taught, encouraged, and pushed for constant high-level effort. Darren watched, taught a little, evaluated, continued his instruction, and assessed some more.

Darren immediately stepped in any time a player made a mistake or a drill was not to his liking. He was on it from the get-go. He yelled, "Stop the drill! Hold the balls." His booming voice required no whistle. Darren believed in correcting players immediately and then repeating the drill until he was satisfied. This was an example of his excellent teaching skills and his sense of urgency to get it right. Teaching and full-speed play dominated the two-hour practice.

As the first official practice's end neared, Darren walked past Coach Mays and whispered, "These girls have been taught very little. It looks as if they have never had consistent, structured practices."

"Coach, these girls only know one thing: losing. This is gonna take some time and patience," said Mays. Darren kept pacing the sidelines.

The practice moved into a five-on-five scrimmage, the last component of the day. Tiffany, the expected starting center, had been in the doghouse since the starting whistle. The coaches did not put her on the court for the scrimmage. The message was loud and clear; no one said a word.

As the scrimmage played out, the ladies tiredly pushed on. They had never gone this hard for this long. To no coach's surprise, only Crowe and Peck had something left in the tank. Those two were handling the high-level intensity with determination. The coaches verbally rewarded their effort and watched as each player on the floor was inspired to fight through their fatigue.

Finally, the horn sounded, calling an end to the first practice. Most of the team was out of breath, covered in sweat, and visibly exhausted. Even so, Darren called the girls into the center circle to start the Well-Better-How (WBH) exercise. It was a method Jimmy had: "I do it after every presentation. It has helped me realize there is no perfection—always room to improve."

Darren began, "Okay, what was one thing we did well today? Anyone?" No one responded, so Darren followed up, "This is a safe place. I want to hear your thoughts."

"I thought we got better as the practice went longer," said Vivian.

"We adjusted well with the new drills," said Tiana. "Some of those drills I've never done before."

"Good," said Darren. "Now, where do we need to improve?" he asked.

"We need to be in better shape," said Patricia. Crowe was fearless in speaking her mind, once again showing her natural leadership abilities.

"And how are we going to improve?"

"Just need to keep doing the work," said Vivian.

Darren offered his final thought, "Overall, we did a good job. However, we need to correct one thing immediately, and that is how we enter the practice. Virtually everyone walked onto the court. Let me remind you—practice begins when you come through those doors over there." Darren pointed toward the doors. The team turned their heads to look. "Which means you need to lock right in. Run onto the floor. Give 100 percent. When you exit those doors, practice ends, but not until then. This goes for me and my coaches too."

"Coaches, do you have anything to add?" Darren asked.

Coach Morris spoke up. "Ladies, it's grit, excellence, and commitment. This is what you have decided a Lady Foxhound should look like. We need to see it every day, not just when you feel like it."

Coach Bennett added. "We are only teaching a few things, but we need to be excellent at those things. Remember what Coach was saying. Simplicity and execution."

As the other coaches nodded, Darren called them to close the practice. "Thank you everyone. Dominique, you have the honor to break us down today."

With everyone's hands touching above their heads, she called out 1-2-3, and in unison, they all yelled, "Hounds."

The team jogged off the court to the doors exiting the floor.

As pleased as Darren was with their practice, he still had two issues: one being Tiffany Hitchcock, and the second defining when practice actually begins and ends. Darren sent a quick text to Tiffany: *"Meet me in my office tomorrow at 2:24 p.m."* She responded almost immediately with a thumbs-up. Darren then reached out to Jimmy. *"Please meet me tomorrow at the Pic & Pac at 7:31 a.m. Need some advice."*

Reflecting on his early strategy session with Jimmy that morning, Darren's thoughts were interrupted when, at 2:20 p.m., Tiffany walked into his office—well, it was more of a painful shuffle. He knew the practice had worked her hard, even if she hadn't put 100 percent into it. The glass-paned basketball offices were wide open—there would be no hiding behind a desk or a door. Transparency was evident, and it was intentional.

"Come in, Tiffany," Darren said. "Have a seat." Coach Mays was situated beside the head coach. In their meeting that morning, Jimmy had advised Darren to always have a staff member with him when he conducted player meetings that involved potential disciplinary action. They were getting an early start on behavioral changes. Jimmy also suggested documenting these conversations and taking notes as they proceeded, so Darren had his coach's notebook splayed on the desk, ready to take meeting notes. It was an act that needed to become a habit.

Wasting little time, Darren looked directly at Tiffany and asked, "Why were you late yesterday?"

Darren leaned back into his desk chair, waiting for her answer. He could see her defiance in her eyes. *Her former coach must have let tardiness slide.*

"I didn't think I was that late to practice." Normally, in the past, Darren would have cut her off at "I didn't." He never let a player talk or explain themselves first. *He* did all the talking. This time, Darren held his tongue. He let her finish.

"You were still talking when I arrived. I was there for all of the drills . . . So, why wasn't I on the first team?"

She is so unaware, Darren realized. And judging by Coach Mays shifting in her seat, Darren didn't think she believed the excuse either. "I started every game last year," Tiffany finished.

Darren paused and took a breath. "Ok, Tiffany. First off, punctuality does not seem important to you. For a long time, I didn't think so either. When I was playing in college, I thought I was the man. Who's to tell me to be someplace at a particular time? Well, I quickly found out that attitude would not fly. I came late one morning. I was only one minute late. It didn't matter. Time was important to my coach. He ran me until I puked, then suspended me from my college's first game. I had to watch from the sidelines—I can still remember how much that sucked. And you can bet that I was on time for everything after that day. It's one of the things I take pride in now." Jimmy had lectured Darren on the importance of always admitting mistakes before criticizing others.

"Being on time is number one in our program—number one. We made it clear in the first meeting, but it's my fault for not hammering home its importance and explaining the consequences of tardiness. Being late meant that you weren't prepared to contribute to the team. Therefore, there are consequences, thus, no scrimmage.

"Meetings are part of the practice. When we set the time, we emailed you and your teammates. We even set up a group chat to confirm. 2:39 p.m. That's when the meeting begins. All our meetings, workouts, practices, departures, you name it, will happen at a specific time. Crazy numbers like 3:31 p.m. or 9:01 a.m.—whatever it may be. Why? Because it is a form of exactness. Time is important. If we were traveling yesterday, you would have missed the bus. There won't be a role call—we'll just leave."

Tiffany's body language said she was not buying it. Darren continued anyway, "I am ok if you are not with us."

It was an ultimatum, the likes of Coach John Wooden, who threatened to kick his star player, Bill Walton, off the team if he didn't get a haircut.

"It's alarming that you are a senior exhibiting this type of behavior. You should be *setting* the example, not becoming the example. I expect more from my seniors. Understand, no one gets special treatment—everyone has to operate within the program's standards, including me and the assistant coaches."

Darren continued, "We will expect you to be on time, do things to the best of your ability, and set the example expected of a senior player." Before Darren dismissed Tiffany, he complimented her. "You have the ability, or you would not be here. Today is a new day—you can choose to be better." There was a pause, then, "What questions do you have for me?" asked Darren.

Tiffany only shook her head that she didn't have anything to say. She stood and walked out, exhibiting the body language of someone defiant and not bought in.

Coach Mays looked at Darren and asked, "She doesn't get it, does she?"

Darren shrugged, "We will see how she reacts. She could turn things around." Privately, Darren wasn't optimistic.

The coaches marched off to meet with the team ahead of day two's practice. The team was gathered and ready to listen by 2:35 p.m., but Coach Mays waited to start. Finally, Tiffany walked in at 2:39 p.m. She was testing the standards.

14 THE GREEN LINE

> *If you don't have time to do it right, when will you have time to do it over?*
>
> —John Wooden,
> Hall of Fame Basketball Coach

🔗 Darren 🔗

Darren had hardly walked into the Pic & Pac when he heard someone calling out to him.

"How did those first practices go, Coach?" Frankie asked, clutching his oversized coffee mug with both hands.

"Oh, like most first days—we need a lot of work," Darren said. "And I haven't forgotten about y'all. I will speak with Dr. Harding about the Foxhound Phanatics attending a practice or two." Frankie and company looked pleased. Madie strolled over to the coach, bringing the coach his coffee and his favorite pastry, the seasonal pumpkin scone.

"You wanna come to watch a practice?" Darren asked.

"Luv to," she said. "How we lookin'?"

"Not great. It's a big adjustment for the ladies. It will take time to get unanimous buy-in."

Jimmy arrived moments later and immediately asked how the first day went.

"We were just okay. Not enough energy or enthusiasm. Definitely not ready for a game. They walked onto the court. It took all my self-control not to send them home. All except for Crowe and Peck. It's another level with those two." Darren paused, noticing how Jimmy listened with his full attention and no judgment. "There I was, a nervous wreck, my first actual practice in a hundred years, and these ladies acted like . . . Hell, it was no big deal—utterly lazy. Showing up is not enough. I shoulda put them on the baseline and ran the shit out of them." Darren just shook his head.

"You've coached professionals, Darren. They're at a different level. If they don't produce, they're out—they'll get someone else. It's a different story here. Here, it is about self-discipline and motivation—organizing the development of your team and becoming the leader they deserve." Jimmy was quick to offer Darren some encouragement.

Darren nodded, "That's true, Jimmy, but these girls do need to know that practice is as important as the games—even more important. I've got to drill that into their friggin heads somehow."

Jimmy put both hands up as if to slow down Darren's thought process. "Just take a breath. It's day one. Learning that practice should be highly valued is a task. This won't be easy. These players know nothing about winning. Know nothing about preparing or working hard. When I was a young junior college head coach, we had the same problem. But I had a simple approach to get the energy up. I went and got some tape one day—blue painter's tape that's two inches wide. I stuck the tape about 10 feet from the actual court. You couldn't get onto the court without crossing it. Then, I told everyone that the tape signified the start and end of practices. Eventually, we painted a permanent Green Line. Green so that when you cross the line, you're ready to *GO!*"

Darren quickly bought into the idea. "Can we get it done this week?"

"Yes, I will send a message to my guy in the facilities department. It should only take a couple of days."

"One more thing," Darren asked. "Can Frankie Cornell and his group stop by and watch a couple of practices? Madie too? I'll introduce them to the team, maybe get a photo. Fire them up, ya know. Promote the program. Create a little pride."

"Now you're thinking! The true win will be if we can get ole Dr. Bernadette over to watch practice," Jimmy said with a wry smile.

"Maybe we can have the team come here for breakfast for an unofficial meet and greet," Darren suggested. "I know how you feel about getting out into the community."

Jimmy called out to Madie, "Hey, Madie, do you think we can find a spot to put some VCSU photos in here? Maybe a team photo?"

"Bring me sumpin, and I'll finda spot."

Darren was excited to implement the Green Line idea. It was a simple fix that could have some powerful results.

On his way out, Jimmy stopped to say goodbye to Frankie and his crew. "See you fellows over at Lewis . . . 3:31 p.m.— that's when the girls get going. Don't be late." He winked as he walked away.

"Appreciate it, Doc," Frankie said.

This man never stops, Darren thought, *and I really should have brought my journal today.* "Habits, Darren, habits," he mumbled to himself.

At 2:36 pm, the ladies entered the meeting room and were given something new—the Green Line lecture. More changes.

As each Foxhound walked in, Darren handed them a sheet explaining the Green Line principles."When you cross the Green Line, practice begins," Darren said. "You must be ready to work. Embody that grit, excellence, and commitment. Only then can we improve. Practice ends when you cross the Green Line. From 3:31 p.m. to 5:31 p.m., we expect your best."

Just as the oddly specific times provided consistency and exactness, so would the Green Line. Only then could they make the best use of their time.

During practice, Coach May stuck the painter's tape as you exited the doors that separated the court and the hallway to the locker room. Soon, a permanent Green Line would take its place. Darren was pleased to see that day two was much improved. Practice intensity was noticeably better. Darren and his staff were making small gains. The players were adjusting to change, and it was only the beginning.

15 PRAISE

> *I've learned that people will forget what you said, people will forget what you did, but people will never forget how you made them feel.*
>
> —Maya Angelou,
> Writer and Presidential Medal
> of Freedom Recipient

⚔ Darren ⚔

Jimmy had told Darren that one of the biggest mistakes he could make would be to overwork the players. This less-is-more theory seemed counterproductive to Darren. Less was less to him. Still, practices moved into the middle second week; the coaches kept pushing the team and raising the standards. Still, Darren was worried the team was falling behind. They were below the line of acceptable in his book. He was hard to please.

One day, Darren talked to his staff, "I don't know how you have remained in this college game for so long. I feel like we will never be ready to play." The coaches reassured Darren that the foundation should be the priority. Darren heard their support but wasn't comforted. They could only wait and see.

Darren's nerves amplified when he received a text from Jimmy saying that he'd be by to watch the day's practice. No surprise, Jimmy arrived before practice began.

"Dr. Harding, it's a pleasure to have your presence." The words felt stiff, but Darren was trying to keep it professional.

"Happy to be here. I do want to speak with you after practice. Your assistants can run today's post-practice film session. It'll be good to let them run the show today. That's called delegating," Jimmy said with a sarcastic tone.

"Okay, smartass," Darren dropped the formality with a smile.

The day's practice was slightly above the line. It was a relief to Darren to finally get some acceptable results. Hitchcock was being pushed by 6'4" freshman Alicia Knox. The Wilson sisters were gaining on the inconsistent Slade and Davis. Crowe and Peck were their usual selves: gritty and competitive, with high-level motors. The rest of the team just tried to keep up. After the coaches dismissed the team, the players all jogged off the court, crossing the painted Green Line before slowing to a walk.

Darren turned to Jimmy. "What did you think of the practice?"

"The team is shaping up nicely. And Crowe, she's special," Jimmy was quick to move on to the next lesson. "Have you ever heard of the great Charles Schwab?"

Darren shook his head, wondering where this story was headed.

"He's a former steel mogul, someone who became one of the first Americans to earn over a million dollars a year. He was paid a record salary because of his people skills. Schwab once said, 'I consider my ability to arouse enthusiasm among my people the greatest asset I possess . . . and the way to develop the best in a person is by appreciation and encouragement.'[3] He also knew that criticism was a killer of ambition, especially when it's delivered by superiors."

"Where was this advice 10, 20, 30 years ago?"

Jimmy laughed at Darren. "You never would have listened. Who are you kidding? Anyway, like Schwab, praise the players and their efforts. Show your appreciation. When they do the right thing, notice and make it public. Encourage them to keep at it. Make them feel important. Take Patricia. She's the ideal Lady Foxhound and would run through a wall if you said that was a drill. So start with her. If she ramps it up a notch, the rest of the team will respond. Praise is not just for those who struggle. We all need it."

Darren knew he was learning from someone with exceptional people skills. "Thank you for taking the time, Jimmy. I'll get to work on that next."

Later that evening, Darren sent Crowe a text message: *"Trish, can you meet me in my office tomorrow at 10:32?"*

A few minutes later, she responded, *"Sure, Coach. See you then."* The text was far less enthusiastic than her usual responses. Darren realized she may be expecting a scolding. He sent another text seconds later, *"All is good. Just a quiet chat, you're not in trouble. Have a good night. See you tomorrow."* Darren's awareness was improving.

🏀 🏀 🏀

Darren was diving into the deep end of the pool with this kind of meeting; most of his past solo conversations were about problems, either attitude issues or off-the-court incidents. Those meetings frequently became contentious.

Darren's office was a short walk from the auditorium lobby. Initially, Darren struggled with the transparency of its glass walls, but it was his norm now. At 10:04, Patricia Crowe came walking down the hallway. Darren saw her and walked to the door.

"Come in, Trish," he said. "Grab a seat."

"Nice hoodie, Coach," Crowe said, pointing at his new VCSU merch.

"We just got these in," Darren said, "along with a ton of other things. The university just signed a contract with LuLu. You ladies will get some 'swag,' as you young people call it. They'll be filling your lockers up soon enough. The president wants us to look first-class."

"Look great, feel great, play great," Crowe echoed.

"Exactly. You get it, Trish. That's why I wanted to bring you in and tell you that you are a wonderful player. I have enjoyed coaching you these past couple of weeks. And you may not notice it, but the others gravitate toward you. Keep setting the example and raising that standard." Darren said all of this as he made eye contact.

"Thank you, Coach. Means a lot to hear that, especially from someone who has coached at the highest level."

"One more thing, Trish," added Darren.

"Yes, sir?"

"I need my best player to be my hardest worker—and this is why. If you are the hardest worker, we will be a better team. Lead and be vocal if you feel comfortable. Let the vocal part be natural. Unapologetic. I'll correct you on the court, but if I need to criticize you, I'll bring you into the office. You have to be a visible leader to the team."* Darren felt good about their talk. "Do you have any questions?"

"No," Crowe said, "I'm good, Coach. See you at practice." As she closed the door and left, Darren saw her walking towards the lobby, standing tall and walking with new confidence. *How has it taken me so long to learn that praise may work better than criticism?*

Darren pulled out his calendar and scheduled individual player meetings for the next two weeks. He vowed to send text messages of praise to players who were pushing themselves and setting the example. The starting five—Peck, Davis, Hitchcock, and Slade—were first up on the calendar.

---

* Legendary football coach Vince Lombardi often heavily criticized Bart Starr in front of his Green Bay Packers teammates. Finally, Starr asked to meet with Lombardi in his office after practice. Bart explained to his coach that he could not be chewed out in front of the very men he was supposed to lead. "If I've got a chewing out coming, fine, but do it in the privacy of this office where you apologize to me when you know you're wrong. Otherwise, don't ever expect me to go out there and be your leader," Starr said, according to an NFL Films retrospective, adding, "And he never, ever raised his voice to me again."

16 | VULNERABILITY

> *Truth and courage aren't always comfortable,*
> *but they're never weakness.*
>
> —Dr. Brené Brown,
> Author and Podcast Host

⚒ Darren ⚒

After three weeks, it was pretty obvious who was putting in the real work and who on the team was simply faking it. Most coaches know that anyone can grind for a couple of weeks. But once the work gets tough, the players who aren't fully committed would start to show their true colors. Darren and his staff were already seeing the signs. Darren knew it was time for another chat with Jimmy.

Sitting in a booth at the Pic & Pac, Darren was anxious as he waited for Jimmy, even as Madie peppered him with questions. He answered all of them but kept one eye on Jimmy. Ever the approachable president, Jimmy worked his way through the crowd, exchanging greetings, shaking hands, and posing for pictures until he finally took his place beside Darren.

"Dr. Harding, welcome. Can I get ya sum coffee?" asked Madie. "Coach got to tell'n me all 'bout that NBA, but I guess I betta get on wit my day."

"The NBA? Was she asking you about the incident?" Jimmy didn't waste time dancing around a sensitive subject.

"Yup. She walked up and asked what happened in New York that night—what was going through my head. It was outta nowhere. Caught me off guard. She knew most of the details though, had Googled it. But I told her the rest. I wouldn't dare disappoint Madie!"

Jimmy nodded, "I was just thinking the other day that you should come clean about the Christmas Day meltdown. Tell the team what happened—they've already heard stories, so why not be honest with your side? Take accountability. Be vulnerable."

"Jimmy, what good would telling the team do?"

"You recognize the name Dr. Brené Brown?"

"I can't say that I do."

"Well, she has one of the most watched Ted Talks on YouTube.[4] It's about being vulnerable. By opening up to the team, being honest with them, you will become more than a coach—they'll see you as a person. It'll develop trust. Who knows, they may open up and tell you something from their past. Something difficult that's changed them. It will be a good relationship exercise."

Darren sipped his coffee as he thought over Jimmy's suggestion. "Okay, I'll give it a try." In the back of his mind, though, Darren was scared to death to open up.

Later that day, Darren asked the staff about the Christmas incident. They knew the major details—the salacious details from Hack's writing and discussions on social media. Coach Mays, in particular, made it clear she thought a team discussion was warranted.

Darren was nervous to open up. It was never his strength. In fact, regardless of what Jimmy had told him, he still was not convinced that being vulnerable would show strength. But Jimmy always had his best interest at heart. Darren wanted to get it off his chest and see what happened.

As the next pre-practice meeting room filled with staff and players, Darren took a deep breath and exhaled, steadying himself. As someone who typically dominated meetings, practices, and games, this was outside of his comfort zone.

Darren began, "You probably don't know that I grew up about an hour north from here. Culpeper. I was the starting point guard all of high school. My coach was tough, screamed a lot. It seemed to work, though, because we won.

"Then I went to Emory & Henry University. No scholarships. Small school. It put a chip on my shoulder. My college coach was even more demanding, but we won. So, again, it clearly worked. After Emory, I spent five years as a graduate assistant and assistant coach at Randolph-Macon.

"That's when I got a break. I had a player, Nick Vasho, who was a DIII All-American. Let me tell you, he was scouted by every NBA team. That's how I met a Chicago Bulls scout. They needed a new assistant coach, and I impressed him. I spent 10 years in Chicago and became one of the top assistants. The Knicks came calling—hired me as their new head coach. I was one of the youngest head coaches to ever be hired by an NBA franchise. We won an NBA championship in my fifth year. That's when my ego exploded.

"The pressure mounted. I adopted a win-at-all-costs attitude. Relationships got tense, both with my athletes and coaches. I started drinking. After games and practices—really, whenever I was alone. As the seasons went by, the team got worse, and so did my attitude. We started on a losing streak—couldn't shake it off. Each season, I felt like a failure, so I pushed myself harder. Pushed the team harder. Then, on a Christmas Day game, I lost it. I became totally unglued over a horrendous call from the referee. Straight-up punched him. Of course, I got ejected. I left the arena, fuming mad, and immediately drove to a bar. Spent a few hours drinking. Driving home, I totaled my car and was arrested. Spent the night in jail. It's no surprise I was fired the next day after 10-plus seasons as New York's head coach. Humiliating. There were AA meetings, counseling sessions, and community service.

"Through some blessing, I got a job at a junior college soon after being fired, but I wasted that chance. I was still bitter and mad. There were few happy days. I lasted less than a year. Then the rejections came—no one wanted me, and that was a real blow. I finally decided it was time to do the work, self-reflecting and such. It was one of the hardest times of my life, but I was turning things around. Then, soon after, Dr. Harding called and offered me this job. My third—and likely final—chance. I am lucky to be here and excited to be your coach."

Darren let his words hang in the air, then asked, "What questions do you have for me?"

Sophomore guard Vivian Peck quietly asked, "Do you drink anymore?" Darren wasn't surprised, even if the rest of the team was silent.

"No, Vivian. I am an alcoholic. So only water and a lot of coffee." A few smiles followed.

The team sat frozen as they took in their coach's story. Darren was surprised to feel a sense of calm—a sense of safety—after sharing so much of his life. A few players thanked him for sharing as they left the meeting room. Darren thought he could see respect and empathy in their eyes—not judgment as he had feared he'd find.

As they moved onto the court, Darren let his staff push the players. He observed, offering advice when necessary but mostly sitting back. Taking it all in.

The season was fast approaching. *Would we be ready?* It was too early to tell, but Darren was starting to feel hopeful. He certainly felt better about being vulnerable.

17 STOP-START-CONTINUE

I don't want my emotions to get the best of me. I want my emotions to bring out the best in me.

—Coach Mike Krzyzewski,
Hall of Fame Basketball Coach

✍ Darren 🏀

Emotions run high in sports. Darren Blood's emotions used to get the best of him. But he was now a work in progress.

As grateful as he was, Darren didn't quite understand why Jimmy Harding had taken on the arduous task of mentoring him, but Darren could already feel the difference: The work together was slowly shrinking the emotional curve that produced behaviors unworthy of his skill and passion for basketball. With an exhibition game looming and the regular season just around the corner, there was too much on the line. It was time to take another step toward personal improvement for the good of the team and program.

Darren was painfully aware of how much hung on this first game. Although it was only an exhibition game, the nation would be watching. He'd have to keep his obnoxious courtside behavior in check. First impressions were more important.[5]

Many in Eagle Gap, at VCSU, and the broader basketball world would be seeing him in action for the first time in years. Thanks to Gene Hack and YouTube, Darren knew his hire was still somewhat controversial.

Jimmy had sat Darren down, though, and gave him one of those famous pep talks with a dose of reality: "It was unbearable to watch your sideline demeanor before. You sulked. That bad body language soaked your team with negativity. You can't do that with the Lady Foxhounds or they'll quit on you. It's time to show everyone, including the Gene Hacks of the world, the work you've put in. Embody the mindset of Hall of Famer head basketball coach Dean Smith. He's known for his ability to control his emotions during a game. Unshakable, even when things weren't going his team's way. He was always in control of his emotions."[6]

Thankfully, Jimmy had yet another exercise to help Darren regulate courtside: a Stop-Start-Continue list.

Darren ran through the strategy as he made his way to the pre-practice meeting. *First step: Pick one thing I can stop, one I can start doing, and one thing I can continue to make a positive impact. Write them down as reminders. Short-term fixes for long-term behavior changes. Chasing that positive impact. Reset and make the adjustments (MTA).*

Darren knew his stop list was long, but he would take it one step at a time, starting with something he had struggled with since he was a young boy—trying to control the uncontrollable. Darren's start list was to delegate more. He'd continue doing what he did best: teaching the game.

Jimmy had even suggested that Darren use the exercise with the team, providing the chance for players to open up and be a little more vulnerable, which may even help bring the team closer. It would also force each player to reflect and improve. As the coaches waited for the team to arrive, Darren ran through the exercise and asked them their thoughts. "Love it," Coach Mays said. The others nodded in agreement and decided to participate as well.

Darren felt ready and more comfortable speaking about his shortcomings—a true sign of personal growth.

"Ok, ladies. Today, we have a new exercise for you called Stop-Start-Continue. This is some Dr. James Harding wisdom I'm sharing with you. Now, you all should have your journals with you." In a flash, Jayla Horn and Hailey Broyles shot out of their seats and ran to the door. Both had forgotten their journals. Darren let it go. Horn and Broyles were back in less than a minute.

Looking at Jayla and Hailey, Darren sarcastically asked, "Are we ready now?" A few giggles and smiles followed. Without even realizing it, Darren was connecting with his team. He moved on, instructing the team to make their lists.

After three minutes, each player had their Stop-Start-Continue. Darren asked who would be willing to share their "Stop." Patricia Crowe raised her hand and said, "I am going to stop worrying about what other people say or think about me." A telling statement—and a clear indication of who their leader was—a great leader who is not worried about what others think or say.

Vivian Peck went next. "I need to stop being distracted by social media and be more present with what I am doing."

Darren followed, "There is your start, too, being present. I think we all could be better at that. I know I could."

"How about you, Alicia? What do you need to stop?"

"Staying up too late. I am exhausted during the day," said the freshman center.

Other stops included eating too much junk food, procrastinating, playing video games, being too negative, and overusing their cell phone. They moved on to starts, which centered on basketball (foul shots, defense, and rebounding) and interpersonal development (active listening, being more positive, and calling home more). Some of their "Continue" goals were to focus on improving every day in every way, in particular, becoming a better teammate.

Darren was pleased with the participation and closed the meeting by sharing his own choices: "I need to stop trying to control what I can't control, start delegating more to my staff, and continue to teach basketball at the highest level with the highest expectations—even for myself." Inspired by Darren's example, his staff followed suit, sharing their own lists. It was a productive meeting, and they headed into practice with a newfound focus.

🐾 Jimmy 🐾

The next day, Jimmy got a flurry of texts about the exercise from Darren. *"It was a hit. All the coaches said it was a smash that brought the team closer together. Can't wait for the next one."* Jimmy smiled, satisfied that his protege was committing his all to EQ coaching.

Lurking on the horizon was a real opponent to test the Lady Foxhounds, but, more importantly, an opportunity for Darren to make a great first impression. He knew he only had one chance.

18 FIRST IMPRESSION

> *We don't know where our first impressions*
> *come from or precisely what they mean, so*
> *we don't always appreciate their fragility.*
>
> —Malcolm Gladwell,
> Author and Journalist

🪃 Darren 🪃

Branding at the collegiate level is critical. It's hard to sell a losing program, but selling a program with a controversial ex-NBA coach . . . easy. Jimmy had told Darren that the hottest-selling T-shirt read, "These Foxhounds are out for Blood." The team loved it. So much so, they wore it in pre-game warm-ups. Surprisingly, Darren liked it too. He knew that many were critical of Harding for choosing him. However, his president embraced the controversy with boldness—a true sign of a great leader. Jimmy was used to the boss role and could make the tough decisions. "There's no point fearing what others think," Jimmy had said to Darren. "I believed hiring you was the right decision."

As the new season progressed, Darren saw bobbleheads, gift packs, and local business giveaways crop up, all in support of him and the Lady Foxhounds.

Darren's nerves intensified as the first game approached. Although it was only an exhibition game, this wouldn't be some glorified scrimmage. It felt more significant since Darren would have to make his controversial debut. Darren could feel all eyes on him, both when he ventured into the small town of Eagle Gap and with the corresponding national media.

Darren and his staff had scouted their opponent, DIII Roanoke College. It was a school with a rich basketball tradition. With five straight winning seasons and as annual contenders in the Old Dominion Athletic Conference, Virginia Central State had a challenge ahead of them.

As the girls ran out for pregame warm-ups, Darren took a minute to assess the auditorium. He was pleasantly surprised by the size of the crowd—nearly 3,000 fans. Even the mascot, Sampson, was there in a VCSU sweater. People could pose with the honorable dog for only $5.

The starting five, made up of Vivian Peck, Patricia Crowe, Ruby Davis, Dominique Slade, and Tiffany Hitchcock, was expected. These five players had been playing the longest, but the coaches had a feeling this was not their best five—it was still very early. The three freshmen, Alicia Knox and the Wilson twins, were pushing to play. They were hard workers, appeared coachable, and seemed to embrace the newly established Foxhound traits. With warm-ups done, Darren and the coaches entered the locker room for one last talk with the team. "I am not worried about what Roanoke does. My only concern is our execution, effort, and focus. It's simple: We have to get more shots than they do, and we have to get *better* shots.[7] This statement was the core of the Lady Foxhounds' overall strategy. On defense, make them as uncomfortable as possible. Communicate and provide weak-side help. On offense, move the ball, move without the ball, be physical with our screening, and create as many mismatches as possible. Find a body after the shot is taken. Take good shots."

As Darren walked alone to the court, he said quietly to himself, "Be the leader, teach, be patient, set the example, and have fun." Sports psychologists have often found that positive talk yields positive results. Darren could not listen to his doubts, or he'd fall into that negativity trap. He was doing his best to improve every day.

From the start of the game, it was clear the Foxhounds were better than Roanoke. The Hounds jumped to a 12–2 lead in the quarter's first five minutes. Even though the team showed incredible improvement since their first practice scrimmage, some bad habits quickly resurfaced. They were often impatient on offense, forcing a bad shot or making a poor pass into traffic. Slade and Davis were lazy when getting back on defense—this allowed two easy baskets from Roanoke. But Darren did not pull them off the court. Each time there was a mistake, he took a breath and a sip of his water bottle to remain calm. Darren knew all eyes were on him, and he had to perform too. Although he stood several times to shout instructions, he kept his frustration in check.

The first quarter ended with VCSU ahead, 20–12. All five starters had remained on the court for the entire quarter. They were fatigued when the horn sounded; even Trish wasn't immune. It was the first time they had pushed so hard. Darren and his staff had been emphasizing conditioning for weeks, but this was clear proof they needed to grind every day to develop that stamina.

The second quarter began with five different athletes on the court: guards Hailey Boyles and Kelsey Kurtz, the Wilson twins as forwards, and Alicia Knox at center. Darren was mimicking the great Dean Smith and his Blue Team approach. By playing an entirely new set of five, they could spell the starters for a few minutes. And Darren knew the players wouldn't see themselves as lesser-than but recognize the pride in serving such an important role. His Foxhound Five locked into the game like a hound on a trail. When the horn sounded, the halftime score sat VCSU 36–Roanoke 28.

After speaking with his staff to get their input, Darren addressed the team. "We moved the ball on offense and got some good looks. Let's crash those boards on offense a little better. The defense was good, but it could be better. Agree?" Darren paused for effect. The team, in unison, agreed, some verbally while others nodded. Only two players seemed disengaged—Hitchcock had her head down, and Slade was looking away. Darren pushed on: "Show some toughness and finish! You have control over the next 20. No one else . . . Coaches, anything to add?"

Coach Mays commended the Foxhound Five for their efforts, and Coach Alexander asked for better communication on defense. Darren's mind raced, but he controlled himself— voice calm and body language steady. *Not something NBA Coach Blood could have done. He would have been critical of what went wrong without praising what went right. He would have crushed any spirit that was left.* Darren smiled, knowing he was making small gains alongside the team.

The second half was not as close as the first. The Foxhounds pulled away from the start of the third quarter and went on to win 82–59. Crowe was magnificent, scoring a game-high 24 points. Point guard Peck dished out 12 assists. The rest of the team gave 100 percent, and that was all Darren could ask for. The other three starters, Slade, Davis, and Hitchcock, had clear lapses in focus. The lack of overall hustle was evident. Darren knew old habits were hard to break, and they still had work to do. Darren ushered the team to the locker room but took a moment to glance around. Fans seemed overjoyed with the victory as they filed out of the auditorium. President Harding and Darren had been working in the shadows to rebuild the women's basketball program. Few had seen the team perform until tonight. *And it was a good first impression.*

Darren's high from their success only lasted a short time. After watching the entire game film, Darren checked his emails before bed. Instant anxiety: There was an email from Academic Services, subject line "Tiffany Hitchcock—Academic Performance."

What now?!

19 I NEED TWO SOLUTIONS

> *Change the changeable, accept the unchangeable, remove the unacceptable.*
>
> —Dr. Kevin Elko,
> Motivational Speaker and Author

✎ Darren ✎

Tiffany Hitchcock was failing two courses and struggling in the other three. She had attended only about half of her classes. *This girl is unreal*, Darren thought to himself after speaking with Academic Services. The news he received was disappointing but not surprising. Tiffany had never excelled as a student, but she got by. *Where did the communication between Academic Services and our program break down? How did things get this bad?*

In Darren's world, getting by was not enough. The "above the line" work is what separates good from great.[8] Demanding excellence on the court was one thing, but academics was a new issue for him. There wasn't an NBA requirement to pass Advanced Statistics or Governmental Policy. Darren had struggled in college too and was not a regular on the Dean's List, but he certainly never failed courses.

Following Jimmy's advice, Darren called on his assistant coaches. He was especially upset at Coach Alexander, who was in charge of monitoring academic progress. Darren would deal with him separately.

They met at 10:31 a.m. to discuss Tiffany Hitchcock's situation. The coaches weren't meant to meet until the afternoon, but they had to make the adjustment. When things went sideways, *MTA it*. Get past the problem and move on to the solution.

"Before we talk about anything else, we need to address the issue with Hitchcock." No one seemed surprised. "I believe she has not lived up to our standards from day one. On the court, she has been average at best, and now she's failing two courses and skimming by in the other three." Darren paused, "This is unacceptable. Let me know what you think the solution should be."

No one said anything at first.

Darren knew his old-school way would have been to run Hitchcock in the early hours of the morning until she puked, run the entire team and make her watch, or both, then add an expletive-laced tongue-lashing to her, the team, and anyone within earshot. He knew Jimmy would not approve—it was an autocratic strategy that only produced short-term results. Darren's past explosive outbursts had never proved successful in the long run. They needed to deliver a respectful but firm message to Hitchcock and the team.

Coach Bennett began, "I say we bring Tiffany in and ask her what the issue is, how we got here, and how we can fix it. She's basically broken every standard we've set. Let's be blunt for a second: Tiffany is selfish. I say we suspend her for the first game."

"It'll send a message," said Coach Morris.

"Coach Alexander, what are your thoughts on the matter?" Darren asked, hoping he would take accountability for not being more aware of Tiffany's struggles.

"Coaches, I came up short here. I definitely wasn't on top of this and need to do a better job." Darren nodded and felt his temperature cool.

"What do you think, Coach Mays?"

"Tiffany has had zero good examples or role models before now. No structure, no leadership from the previous coaching staff. This trickles down to the team and demolishes every player's attitude—the team had a losing attitude. We've asked more from Tiffany and her teammates in two months than their previous seasons. People need more than two months to break bad habits. And she is not the only one—there will be more."

Darren thought about it. "We are demanding excellence daily. It is uncomfortable. I see your point. Any other thoughts on the matter?"

Giving him another opportunity to solve the problem, Darren asked, "What do you think, Coach Alexander?"

Coach Alexander spoke up. "I want to apologize again for not staying on top of this. I think we should have Hitchcock apologize to the team for not being the type of player the Lady Foxhounds demand. It will be tough—she'll hate it—but I think it's what she needs to do. That, plus a suspension, will send the right message."

"Agreed. I will bring her in this afternoon to discuss the situation," said Darren. The meeting's focus now turned to the team. They reiterated the basics, "Continue to teach. Be positive. Stick with the process. No letting up," Darren stressed. The first real game was days away.

One thing was decided: Hitchcock would be relegated to the second team for upcoming practices.

As the meeting concluded, Darren sent a quick text to Jimmy asking to meet and discuss the Hitchcock situation. Jimmy responded a heartbeat later, *"I'll call you shortly."*

Darren wanted to fix the issue immediately and move on—today. He sent word through Coach Alexander for Hitchcock to stop by his office at 2:17 p.m. This would allow plenty of time before their 2:39 p.m. pre-practice meeting.

"So Darren, what can I do for you?" asked Jimmy.

"We have an issue I want you to weigh in on. Hitchcock is struggling academically—failing two courses and not doing much better in the others. Class attendance is also an issue. What are your thoughts?" asked Darren.

"Hmmm . . . Well, this is what I would do. Bring her in and ask her to give you two solutions to the problem. She created it, so let's see if she can solve the problem herself."

Darren liked the idea of giving Tiffany the opportunity to solve it.

Jimmy added, "I heard a saying from sports psychologist Dr. Kevin Elko: 'Change the changeable, accept the unchangeable, and remove the unacceptable.'[9] This is an opportunity to see where Tiffany lands."

Darren had never heard the quote before, but it struck home. He knew he would have once been deemed unacceptable.

Jimmy continued, "This does not warrant a harsh penalty, but it is another strike. You have an excellent opportunity to teach and show some outstanding leadership here. I've seen a few practices—this is not shocking. Tiffany is not your hardest worker, nor is she your best player. Being late, missing classes, and performing poorly in the classroom are against all that we stand for here at VCSU. HUDA HUDE—how you do anything is how you do everything. Tiffany has been the poster child for that acronym. This is your opportunity to convey that you will not tolerate a bad attitude, poor performance away from the court, and less than 100 percent on the court."

"I was thinking of suspending her for one game, or a half, or just not starting her," said Darren. "I have a few ideas."

"That sounds promising, but first, let her give you at least two solutions on how to fix the problem. Then you can impose whatever penalty you feel is best," Jimmy advised. "Secondly, and possibly more importantly, do what I call 'fill her bucket.' We all have a bucket. When it is filled, you feel better— supported. The positivity you provide will add to her bucket. If you are too negative, you take from her bucket. You want Tiffany to leave the meeting understanding the consequences without feeling defeated. Provide positive emotional support, not negative."[10]

"Thank you, Jimmy. I appreciate the help." Darren had asked everyone with skin in the game what they thought. It was time to make a fair, wise, and potentially bold decision.

20 FILLING BUCKETS

🔗 Darren 🔗

Darren and Coach Alexander were already settled behind the desk when Tiffany Hitchcock arrived at 2:17 p.m. Following another piece of Jimmy's advice, Darren had asked Coach Alexander to attend the meeting with him. Not only for a second perspective but also because it was Alexander's lack of attention that allowed the academic issues to spiral.

"So, Tiffany," Darren began, "do you know why you are here?"

"My grades?" Tiffany said.

"Yes, your grades. Not just one or two failing courses—all of them," Darren said. "No judgment here—I was never a great student either. Definitely wasn't prepared for college. Do you know what got me going though?"

"No, what?" she asked.

"Basketball," Darren said. "It was my life. Utterly consumed me. Still, to this day, I'm in love with the sport. Can you tell?"

Tiffany laughed a little. "Yeah, Coach, we can tell. You love to practice."

"My college coach was quick to bench me for my poor academic performance. I couldn't stand to be away from the court, so I had to get right quick. Real quick!" Darren said. "My point, Tiffany, is that we have time to fix this problem. Coach Alexander and I can help, but you have to *want* to fix it. We want you to turn things around, but that won't be enough. *You* must want it."

Darren knew that Tiffany had always skated by. From all accounts, the previous coaching staff ran a loose ship and left him with bad habits to break. The old Coach Blood would've yelled at her to do better, but as the new and improved coach, Darren gave her the chance to speak.

"Give me two solutions to solving this issue." He waited for a response.

Tiffany thought for a minute and then leaned back in her chair. "Well, I can go to my professors to see what I can do to make up the work I missed. Extra credit or something."

"That's a start,"

"Maybe I can get some help for the classes I struggle with the most."

"I can help you get a tutor," Coach Alexander offered.

"Those are two great solutions," Darren said, his positive attitude surprising even himself. Jimmy's influence was evident. "Is there anything else you can do?"

Tiffany was blunt, "Actually go to the classes."

Darren lowered his voice and looked directly at Tiffany, moving a little closer as if to say, *only you and I need to know this.* "You are better than this. As a senior, you should be setting the example instead of *being* the example."

Tiffany nodded her understanding.

Darren continued, "We are a better team with you on the court. But you need to push yourself—in the classroom, sure, but in practice too. You can be so much better than what you've shown us. This is not your best. You have a great opportunity here. You get to play college basketball. Self-discipline is the key here."

"I understand, Coach," Tiffany said, and Darren could tell she meant it.

"I'm glad, but there are some consequences we need to discuss here," Darren said. "When we open our season in Norfolk, Alicia will start at center. You will not play the first half."

As the words registered, sadness settled on Tiffany's face. Her shoulders sank. Though he empathized, Darren continued.

"These consequences apply to you and the rest of the team if they fall below the standard we've set. Everyone in the program operates to those same set of standards. Do you understand, Tiffany? We have a team standard." Darren spoke in a fatherly tone, as comforting as possible.

Tiffany nodded, mouth set.

"If you need me for anything, do not hesitate to see me, and I'll do what I can to help," Darren said.

"Can I say something about it at the meeting today?" she asked.

"Of course, you can," said Darren. *Jimmy would be proud of me*, he thought.

After Tiffany left the office, Darren asked Coach Alexander to follow up on her progress every day. If there is any indication of this behavior continuing, Coach Alexander was to let him know so they would handle it immediately.

At the pre-practice meeting, Darren told the team that Alicia would start instead of Tiffany, who would have to sit out due to academic performance. True to his word, Darren said, "Before we begin, Tiffany wants to say something."

The senior stood. She was clearly uncomfortable. Darren gave her a nod of encouragement. Tiffany looked to her teammates and said, "I want to apologize for not handling my responsibilities better. The schoolwork and not going to class . . . I promise I'll step it up."

The team voiced their support and departed on good terms, but Tiffany's body language suggested she was still bothered about the incident. Darren watched as Coach Alexander pulled her to the side.

"Hey, let's put your plan into action," Coach Alexander said. "Talk to the professors, we'll get you a tutor, and you need to start going to the classes. Let me know if you need anything."

"Thanks, Coach," Tiffany said. Her attitude brightened—it just took a little love and support from her coaches.

Darren was proud of Coach Alexander, who seemed more determined than ever to do a better job. Darren knew he wanted to be a head coach one day, and this type of player support would help Coach Alexander reach that goal.

Darren was satisfied with the day's work. Jimmy had told him, "Fill other people's buckets. To gain power, Darren, you need to relinquish it. Fill those buckets. Then they feel good, important, and can enjoy that purpose and meaning. Nurture this, and they'll run through a wall for you."

Darren had latched onto this newest piece of Jimmy's wisdom—that "run through the wall" feeling was his internal compass. A lot of good was happening in Eagle Gap, but there still was a season to play through. On the court, freshman Alicia Knox had the pressure of joining more experienced players on the court, the Wilson sisters were earning their playing time, and the Red Team's identity had gained momentum to the point that the "Foxhound Five" had made it onto T-shirts. Darren knew the work wasn't over; there were omnipresent obstacles that always appeared, but it was up to him to tackle them as they came and keep morale up. He was starting to live up to being the big dog.

BE A LEVEL 10

Darren

Darren had left his journal in the office, so he scrambled back to get it before his morning meeting with Jimmy. *Always have the journal,* Darren reminded himself. The journal was quickly filling up with notes. It was a staple in his preparation.

As Darren entered Lewis Auditorium on the way to his office, he heard voices, sneakers screeching, and the thud of basketballs. "It can't be." Darren couldn't help but say the words aloud. The day before the first game, players working out at 6:45 a.m.? Darren peeked at the court: Crowe, Peck, Davis, Knox, the Wilson twins, and a few of the Foxhound Five were running drills. Here was the unrequired work the coaches had been preaching. *Where were Hitchcock and Slade?* Their absence wasn't totally unexpected. Still, Darren loved what he saw. Crowe and Peck were leading the pack and bringing others with them.

The Pic & Pac faithful greeted Darren with a few autograph chasers as he strolled through the doors. As he signed various memorabilia they presented him with, he thought, *Man, one exhibition game win and they want to get my signature!* Jimmy arrived incognito in his VCSU hoodie and blue jeans. He skated by the crowd unnoticed and sat down across from Darren in their usual spot. Madie saw them and hustled to get coffee. Darren opened by asking, "How is Madie always so quick to get our coffees?"

Jimmy laughed, "Because she is what I call a level 10 leader. Let me tell you about Madie. She always has a great attitude. Have you ever been here and not seen Madie smiling?"

"Nope," Darren said. "And I'm betting it isn't because she feels perfect every day."

"No way. It's impossible. Everyone has problems: you, me, your players, even Madie. But you'd never know it. She is always positive. On top of that, Madie takes pride in what she does. She makes everyone feel important—she fills people's buckets, as well as cups of coffee. She greets every customer with a smile, takes their order, serves slices of pie, tops off their coffees—whatever they need. And you feel good when you leave. That's why customers always come back. Madie is about action and intention. Ask yourself this, Darren," Jimmy said as he leaned back in his chair. "If Madie was not as friendly, never smiled, never checked on your table, would you be inclined to make Pic & Pac your regular stop instead of the other restaurants in town? I'm guessing not. *That's* level 10 leadership. We can learn a lot from watching Madie."

Darren was feverously writing it all down. *BE LIKE MADIE!*

"And hey, make sure you drop off some gear the next time you're here. And don't send an assistant," Jimmy added. "Madie deserves that respect."

"Madie is great," Darren reflected. "I can continue to be better with others. Be more like Madie."

Frankie Cornell made his way to the table.

"Hey, Frankie," said Jimmy.

"I wanted to stop and say good luck tomorrow night. It's a big one." Frankie paused before asking, "Is your boy Hack going to be there?"

Darren rolled his eyes, wondering if Gene Hack was that desperate to drive all the way to Norfolk to see him. "He just may be."

"Let's get that first game. It is always the toughest. I'll let y'all go now. Good day, gentlemen." Frankie strolled off to his boys, who were waiting to talk more sports.

Madie returned with their coffee. "You ready for tomorrow? Dem girls ready?" Madie asked. Darren just smiled. "The people are talk'n, Coach. I told 'em. Watch that Crowe. Sump'n else, she is. Real deal."

"Yes. We're ready," said Darren. Madie placed the mugs down on the table. "Want anything else? Homemade pastries are on the way. It's on the house." Madie was filling buckets.

"You're a gem, Madie," said Jimmy.

"Truly, you keep us going," added Darren. Madie smiled and headed off to greet more tables.

"Here's some good news for you, Darren," Jimmy turned back to him.

"Yeah? What?"

"Out of nowhere, I got an email from Dr. Kelly. She's been impressed with the program so far, especially because of what people are saying about you and the team. Even looks forward to seeing a few games this year. You see, people are noticing."

"Wow . . . well, she did say, 'so far,' as if she's waiting for the other shoe to drop, but we'll take it," Darren said.

"That is a good sign. People are noticing. Now, let's review. We are off to a good start. Tomorrow night is the next step in the program's transformation."

"I think we are as ready as we can be for game one," Darren said as Jimmy pulled out his own journal."

"Here is my analysis of where I think we are. On the court, you and your staff are pushing the team hard. It's clearly evident. Even better, your patience with everyone is evident. You seem calm when chaos ensues. Are you actually calm though?" Jimmy asked.

"Sometimes I want to explode, but I just take a deep breath when I feel it coming on. My pre-practice, self-talk walk helps me too."

"I'm proud of you." Jimmy continued, "I've also noticed you delegating to the other coaches. That should help with the stress. Looks like the team has settled into a routine. Clear, consistent work being done."

Darren added, "The Green Line was a game-changer."

"Speaking of games, tomorrow is a big test. This is your chance to show the Gene Hacks and Bernadette Kellys of the world the new you. Coach Darren Blood is here, and he's here to stay."

Darren spoke up. "I feel like I am trying so hard to stay calm that I lose my intensity sometimes. Like if I am not being loud, it means I don't care. Does that make sense?"

"Absolutely. And there is a fine line. Just keep building relationships with your players. Be yourself. This is a long-term transformation for you and the program. Not a quick fix," added a confident Jimmy. "Off the court, we have taken steps to reconnect with the community. People are finding out you are not quite the monster Hack and others make you out to be. Remain visible, even when we struggle. Keep improving those interpersonal skills."

"I've enjoyed it so far. All of the folks here have made me feel welcome. You, Madie, Frankie and the boys. Things are definitely changing for me," said Darren.

Jimmy nodded in agreement. "All of those adjustments are wins, but you need to improve your on-campus presence. Increase visibility going forward. Professors, staff members, and students all need to be connected with the team. The first meeting early in the semester was great, but the momentum halted. Build that rapport. Be visible on campus. Make it a habit to grab lunch in the dining hall—have you done that yet?"

"Only a couple of times," Darren admitted.

"Not enough," Jimmy countered.

"Agreed. We can do more."

Jimmy continued, "Our alumni are another area we need to develop. There are no suites in Lewis, but we have a hospitality room where you can meet alumni after games. I have our marketing and external affairs people on this—I'll keep you posted. Please make it a point to send personal notes to people you meet. A handwritten note means a lot. One or two a day will make a difference. Make it a habit."

Playing the game a different way. Connections, connections, connections, Darren thought.

"Most important is the team's connection. They are buying in—so far. Even with your history, you were still coaching in the NBA. And now you're here at VCSU with more influence than you realize."

Finally, Jimmy addressed the most important issue. "Hitchcock's subpar academic performance cannot happen again. We need to be on top of that. Anyone dragging the team down needs to be addressed. I know Hitchcock, Slade, and Davis have been challenges, but what did you expect from a 3–27 team? These interpersonal relationships are ongoing work. Remember, one size does not fit all. Communicate with all the players, not just overachievers like Crowe and Peck or the loafers like Hitchcock. Each player needs to be valued because each brings value to the team. You must put in the time—tell them and show each of them that they are valued. We need a Level 10 performance from you every day—practices, games, meetings, communication, consistency—everything counts. If you operate at a Level 10, the team will stand a chance."

Darren finished up his notes in the journal. Looking up, he said, "No questions here. Thanks for your assessment, Jimmy. If I think of something, I will call you."

As they exited the Pic & Pac, Jimmy and Darren walked over to some fans, all of whom were wearing VCSU gear. Darren and Jimmy took advantage of the chance to connect with the community. "We will see all of you at the home opener?" Darren asked.

"We can't wait," one gentleman said.

Every step counts, Darren thought to himself as he headed back to campus on the eve of the season opener. Despite his nerves, Darren was feeling confident as he prepared for his first game in a decade. In just a few short hours—6:01 p.m., to be precise, as Jimmy always encouraged him to be—Darren would board the bus to Norfolk. He knew this game would be a telltale sign of the season to come.

SUMMARY OF PART II:
PREPARATION

1. **Keep Your Philosophy Simple and Clear**

   It begins with a vision, assembling the right people, getting a plan of action, and providing an environment where your team can flourish. Then, do the work.

2. **Self-Assess with Well-Better-How**

   Use the Well-Better-How method to assess your performance. Identify what's going well, what needs improvement, and how to improve it. Engage in this daily self-evaluation to stay focused and foster growth.

3. **Promote Exactness with Crazy Numbers**

   Set specific times, like 8:01 instead of 8:00. It's easier to remember, and it promotes exactly what you want in all other forms of communication.

4. **Create a Boundary for Immediate Focus**

   Mark your own Green Line that designates where the work begins and ends. Once you cross that line—enter the field, office, or board room—it is time to focus and be at your best.

5. **Be Vulnerable**

   Be open about your feelings. Admit mistakes and take responsibility to build trust. Vulnerability helps create a safe environment for growth and sharing ideas. It shows your human side, and human qualities win on the field and on the ledger sheet.

6. Use Start-Stop-Continue

Think about what to start, stop, and continue doing to improve. Encourage your team members to perform this exercise often. It gives them a chance to self-reflect and continuously improve their behaviors.

7. Fill Your Team's Bucket

Imagine everyone has a "bucket" of energy. Praise often fills it; criticism and neglect empty it. Keep your team's bucket full to maintain energy and motivation. It provides positive reinforcement and genuine appreciation—while fostering unity.

8. Be a Level 10 Leader

Level 10 leaders consistently lead by example while going above and beyond. They remain calm under pressure, inspire others with positivity, and motivate others to do their best and reach higher goals.

PART II
REFERENCES

1. Marc D. Allan, "Better Than Imagined," *Butler Magazine*, October 20, 2021, https://stories.butler.edu/better-than-imagined/.

2. Elliott Teaford, "Q & A with Lawrence Frank, Clippers President of Basketball Operations," *Daily Breeze*, October 17, 2017, https://www.dailybreeze.com/2017/10/17/q-a-with-lawrence-frank-clippers-president-of-basketball-operations/#.

3. Dale Carnegie, *How to Win Friends and Influence People* (Simon & Schuster, 1936).

4. "The Power of Vulnerability | Brené Brown | TED," posted January 3, 2011, YouTube, 20 min., 49 sec., https://www.youtube.com/watch?v=iCvmsMzlF7o.

5. Rebecca Knight, "How to Make a Great First Impression," Harvard Business Review, September 12, 2016, https://hbr.org/2016/09/how-to-make-a-great-first-impression.

6. King Rice (basketball coach), discussion with author, June 3, 2024.

7. "Bob Knight - Clinic 1: An Approach to Teaching (1983)," posted April 2, 2018, YouTube, 6 min., 10 sec., https://www.youtube.com/watch?v=QCEUXE3Cjag.

8. Urban Meyer and Wayne Coffey, *Above the Line: Lessons in Leadership and Life from a Championship Program* (Penguin Books, 2017).

9. Kevin Elko, "Winning Baseball Language," lecture, ABCA Convention, Nashville, Tennessee, 2020.

10. Tom Rath and Don Clifton, *How Full Is Your Bucket?* (Gallup Press, 2004).

PART III
THE SEASON BEGINS

22 LOSING IS LEARNING

> *We win or we learn, and learning is winning, so we win or we win.*
>
> —Lanny Bassham, Sport Shooter and Olympic Gold Medalist

⚒ Darren ⚒

Donned in headphones, backpacks slung across their backs, the ladies certainly looked the part of winners as they boarded the bus. The coaching staff stressed that these trips were business trips. That meant, mentally, they wanted big body language, visualizing the game, and exuding confidence. Physically, they needed to be ready to compete. Even the rooming list was intentionally addressed. With a few nights away in hotels, this was an opportune time to use a method that Coach Mays suggested—unbeknownst to the team, room assignments would be deliberately rotated. The goal was to get the girls to develop their relationships.

The team gathered in the hotel meeting room not long after they'd settled into their rooms. Darren walked to the front of the group to address them. Despite his calm demeanor, he was completely nervous. The last time he'd been head coach at Okaloosa-Walton, he'd been on an emotional rollercoaster, still reeling from that fateful Christmas Day game. It felt like a lifetime ago for him.

Darren cleared his throat. "Ladies, tomorrow night is a new beginning for VCSU basketball and for everyone involved in the program. But remember, this is one game. It's 40 minutes—one possession at a time. Surrender the result and focus solely on the process. Don't worry about mistakes. We've prepared. You are ready." He paused for effect, never taking his eyes off the team. "When you lay down tonight, visualize being at your best, making the shot, playing smothering defense, and hitting the boards. If you can see it, you can do it. Compete tomorrow. Be relentless. Give 100 percent. Nothing less." In an unusually vulnerable moment, he added, "It's been a long road back, and I am grateful for the opportunity. I am excited to be here with you, and I will see you in the morning. 9:01 a.m. for breakfast—be on time."

The assistant coaches gave a quick reminder that if you planned to leave the room, they should have their VCSU gear on. More importantly, players needed to respect the 11:05 p.m. curfew, which had been a unanimous team decision.

Darren waved goodbye and headed to his room. He loved the road and had even lived in a New York City hotel during the NBA season, enjoying every second of it. *Be consistent.* Darren had to remind himself not to agonize over the game and instead spend the evening grounding himself. He'd never been a good planner, and this flaw made his time in the NBA more difficult than it already was. He spent too much time on the court and in the film room. Worked the coaches too hard. *The more we lost or struggled, the worse it got. But this will be different.* Darren was committed to the changes. Darren reviewed the next day's schedule one last time before bed:

- ⮥ 9:01 a.m.—Breakfast
- ⮥ 11:31 a.m.—Shootaround
- ⮥ 3:31 p.m.—Pre-game meal
- ⮥ 4:11 p.m.—A quick film session on the opponent
- ⮥ 5:01 p.m.—Departure for Norfolk State

ESPNU had picked up the game. Darren knew it was a national news story only because of his history. Jimmy had communicated how big of a deal it was for VCSU to gain this national publicity. Branding was integral in Division I athletics. Darren knew a lot was riding on this game and was glad that Jimmy avoided putting any additional unneeded pressure on him.

Darren knew from the tip-off that the Foxhounds came to play. Peck's skillful ball handling and Crowe's precise shooting indicated that VCSU could seemingly match Norfolk's guard play. The team had worked in the dark, and it showed. Darren gritted his teeth as their weakness on the front line began to show. Slade was getting outmuscled in the post, Davis was inconsistent on offense *and* defense, and Knox was just inexperienced. Norfolk led 18–14 after the first quarter. Darren was at the edge of his seat but remained sitting, barking instructions only when needed. He was slowly getting back into a coaching rhythm.

At the first TV timeout, Darren huddled with the team and voiced his displeasure on the post-play. "We are not playing tough enough on the boards! Too many second shots! And where is the help, side defense? You gotta communicate there! He remained positive, not singling anyone out. "One possession at a time, ladies. Remember what we worked on. Hey, only down four. Let's turn it around and make the adjustments."

The second quarter mirrored the first. The newly founded Foxhound Five—Hailey Boyles, Kelsey Kurtz, Tiana Wilson, Makayla Wilson, and Knox—was disrupted by Slade's foul trouble and Hitchcock's first-half suspension. This forced a smaller lineup with Jayla Thorn and Nora Okoye, the 11th and 12th players on the roster. They entered down five and were subbed out down by seven. The starters finished the half. Norfolk led 33–26 at the break.

At halftime, the coaching staff walked into a locker room a little more triumphant than Darren had anticipated. This was unexpected, considering they trailed Norfolk by seven. Still, Darren remained calm. "We are doing a good job moving the ball, but we took a few bad shots and failed to box out a few times on defense. Gotta prevent those second and third chances. Otherwise, good first half." His assessment was simple. "Coaches, what did you see?"

"We're competing, ladies," Coach Mays said. "I'm proud of your work so far, but we need more, especially down low."

"We are getting outrebounded 23 to 16 and outshot 30 to 24," answered Coach Bennett. Darren thanked them. He turned to the players.

"What did you see?"

Peck was the first to answer, "They are not hustling back on defense, so get your head up and look for me after you get the rebound. We can push it down the floor."

Crowe followed, "25 can't guard me. I can beat her off the dribble all night. Get me the ball."

Darren nodded and said his final piece, "We are going with the same five starters." He glanced at Tiffany—he hadn't promised she would start the second half, but Darren knew she'd assumed she would. It was a character check for the senior center. The early indicator was that she was going to sulk on the bench. As they headed back onto the court and play continued, Crowe and Peck put their hearts into it. No surprise, Tiffany made her displeasure known from the sidelines.

In the second half, the Foxhounds stood toe-to-toe but eventually fell short 67–60. From Darren and his coaches' perspective, a lot of progress was made, but with the team, they made it clear it was still a loss.

The post-game press conference took place immediately following the game. Darren and Patricia Crowe attended. Crowe had scored 29 and was clearly their best player, so the coaches had agreed she should represent the team. Darren mentally prepared himself for the arrogant Gene Hack, who had indeed traveled just to see him play. He knew it was a noteworthy story—an ex-NBA coach making his head coaching debut with a historically dreadful women's program—and Hack was front and center to report on it.

"Gene Hack, *Washington Insider*. Coach Blood, you were last seen roaming the sidelines with the Knicks. How does it feel to coach women's college basketball?" Hack's question raised eyebrows among the other reporters. It was a shot at women's sports and college sports in one blunt sentence.

Darren responded, his tone cool. "Gene, coaching is coaching and always an honor. It was our first game, and I'm proud of the team's efforts. There is still a lot to work on. We will get better. The girls showed that we came to compete. We'll keep getting better."

Hack continued to poke at Darren, trying to get a rise. "Tiffany Hitchcock has been a three-year starter and sat three-quarters of the game today. What's the strategy here?"

Feeling his careful control start to slip, Darren grabbed a water bottle, opened it, and took a sip. "Gene, Tiffany Hitchcock is a veteran, but we have a plan. It was a coaches' decision." He was starting to boil inside.

The press conference continued without incident.

In the locker room, Darren's message to the team was short. "The effort was there, no doubt. I'm proud of you. However, we shot 38 percent, were outrebounded by 12, and committed 18 turnovers. There is plenty to work on. We will watch the game film, adjust, and improve. Great work, ladies. My college coach used to tell us that there is winning and losing, and there is winning and *learning*. Let's learn from this. Keep your heads up." He turned to his coaches. "Coaches, anything to add?"

"Coach is right. We need to learn from this and make the adjustments."

"Thank you, Coach Mays."

The coaches left the room so the girls could shower and change. Jimmy was waiting outside to console him. "Hey, Darren, we played them tough tonight. You made them earn the win. Crowe and Peck were fantastic. The Wilson sisters too."

"Thanks, Jimmy. We need to get more from our front line. And we'll have to address some personality issues," Darren said.

"You didn't think this was going to be easy, did you? I'm proud of you though. I watched you most of the night. You had plenty of opportunities to lose your cool, but you didn't. How was Hack?"

"The usual pain in the ass."

As Jimmy talked, Darren was still thinking about his three players: Davis, Slade, and Hitchcock. Each of the three exhibited behavior not consistent with the team's values: a lack of effort and a bad attitude. Two things they could not tolerate.

Jimmy wished him safe travels. "I will see you at the Pic & Pac on Monday," he told Darren. The two shook hands and parted ways.

Crowe was the last to board the bus—uncharacteristic for her. Darren noticed his star player was unhappy. He sent Coach Mays to check in.

"Just a little team drama. Tiffany threw a fit in the locker room, swearing about how she didn't play much after all her work this year. Crowe was over it. Didn't say anything to them. But Crowe told me how tired she is of their BS when she busts her ass for the team."

Darren understood Crowe's frustrations. She wanted to win and play well. Points didn't matter. She was not "just another guy"—a "JAG," as Darren sometimes described a player's skill level. Another acronym he had picked up from NBA personnel was when a player was an NFU-type player. That stood for "not for us"—Dominque and Tiffany were in danger of becoming NFUs.

As the team loaded up to return to Eagle Gap, Darren thought, *Do we have too many JAGs and NFUs?* They never produced winning teams. But he heard the voice of Jimmy Harding in his head: "Patience, patience, patience." Darren would not have to wait much longer to determine if his instincts were right.

23 SYNERGY AND GRIT

> *I play my best nine, not my nine best.*
>
> —Skip Bertman,
> Hall of Fame Baseball Coach

🐾 Jimmy 🐾

"Synergy, Darren. That's the word of the day," said Jimmy. "The total is greater than the sum of its parts." Darren quickly wrote the word down in his almost-full journal. "That is what you should look for these next weeks before we begin conference play. I saw on Saturday night that we have an excellent young team. Your best five are Peck, Crowe, Knox, and the Wilson twins—Makayla and Tiana. Much better than the team with Davis, Slade, and Hitchcock. You will need those three. Yes, because they have talent and are far better than the rest. But they lack that *IT* factor."

Madie stopped with coffee and added her two cents: "I liked what I saw with those Wilson twins. Giv'em time. Gonna be good. That Knox too."

From across the room, Frankie yelled, "Crowe for player of the year!!!"

"You're right, Madie. They are going to be good," Jimmy said laughingly.

"The total is greater than the sum of the parts," Darren repeated Jimmy's words. "Synergy."

"Exactly," said Jimmy. "We won two national championships with teams that were connected. We were not overly talented, but we played together, for each other. It is hard to replicate. We wanted our five to play like six or even seven. That's the goal, but it takes time."

Jimmy leaned in toward Darren and said, "I watched Slade, Davis, and Hitchcock on Saturday. All three have talent. Anyone can see that. However, talent must have a work ethic to produce results. And from what you've told me and what I've seen, they are not the most motivated nor the hardest workers you have. And it is difficult to win when your two seniors and one junior are fighting the culture-building process."

"I had a few veteran NBA guys older than me who were unmotivated with terrible attitudes. Trust me, I handled it poorly. We never recovered," said Darren.

"Crowe, Peck, and the three freshmen—Knox and the twins—get after it. Eventually, they'll catch those other three. They work. They seem to care more. Coachable," said Jimmy.

"I still like Davis," said Darren. "We are going to need them all to buy in to reach our goals."

"Have you ever read the book *Grit* by Angela Duckworth?"

"I have not," replied Darren.

"Well, it applies here," said Jimmy.

"Grit is one of our core beliefs about Foxhounds," said Darren. "It would make sense to grab a copy and read it."

"Duckworth describes grit as 'Someone who exhibits intense passion plus intense perseverance toward a long-term goal,'" said Jimmy. "Plus, effort counts twice."

"What do you mean?" asked Darren.

"According to Duckworth, to get from talent to achievement, the naturally talented must display intense effort to develop skill, then proceed to take that skill and add intense effort to garner achievement," said Jimmy. "Let me sum it up for you. Effort plus talent equals skill. Skill plus effort equals results. Effort counts twice."[1]

Darren followed, "That's Crowe. She is a prime example of someone with grit. Peck is not far behind. They are so far ahead of the rest of them. And they are slowly bringing those young girls with them. The Foxhound Five is low on talent, but they are determined. Each of those kids wants to contribute to the whole," said Darren.

"I love the Foxhound Five, and I think Crowe is phenomenal. Your challenge, as I see it, is with Hitchcock, Slade, and Davis. They are not part of your best five. I have seen enough basketball to know. They certainly could be, but you need more from them," said Jimmy. He continued, "Pay attention to those attitudes. You saw it with Hitchcock."

"She had a bad attitude from when she didn't start the second half," Darren said. It bled into the team. Her body language was awful. Her play was mediocre at best. The way she acted after the game and all the way home was the epitome of what a bad teammate would do—negative energy, bringing drama where it is not needed."

"That is your challenge right now. It can ruin a team. Fix it with patience and great communication," said Jimmy. "My old man told me once: 'Someone with a bad attitude has a bad attitude about improving their bad attitude.'"

"I'm sure you had to deal with attitudes. What coach hasn't?"

"In all my years of coaching, teaching, and leading, I have always hoped that everyone wants to be great. While playing for me, all of them are motivated, have a great attitude, and bought into the program. It never happened. There will always be one. In our case here, we may have more than one. Possibly three," said Jimmy.

"Tell me how you dealt with it," asked Darren.

"Remember that Dr. Elko quote I gave you a while back? I applied it. I changed a few, accepted a few, and removed a few. My advice to you is to continue to be patient. It is still early. When there is an issue, fix it. Don't let it fester because things can escalate. Stay ahead of it. Communicate with each player. Proceed with a persistence of wanting 100 percent on and off the floor. No exceptions. Team first. And if things do not change, bold decisions will need to be made. But remember where you heard it first. Crowe, Peck, Knox, and the Wilson twins are your best five. Synergy and grit will win. I promise."

THE STANDARD IS THE STANDARD

✎ Darren ✎

She played with a cockiness trimmed in arrogance, filled with fury. She blew through defenses like a tornado moving through a cornfield. Her agenda was always team first. Her I-don't-give-a-damn-kiss-my-ass attitude was infectious. Patricia Crowe was a coach's dream. All coaches say, "If I only had fifteen Patricia Crowe, we'd never lose."

Tiffany Hitchcock was the exact opposite. Even with her evident talent, Tiffany fell short—sometimes, she appeared as if she did not care, and other times, she was a ball hog to the detriment of the team. She had become a borderline nightmare.

After nearly every practice, Darren thought about removing her from the team. Jimmy, ever the sage, said, "We want to be at our best, not our worst. Be patient—no knee-jerk reactions when making radical decisions. Change can be challenging, especially for individuals like Tiffany Hitchcock, who have not previously been held to a high standard," Jimmy said during his mid-week meeting with Darren. "Keep patient. See how Tiffany, Dominique, and Ruby handle themselves going forward. Understand things always have a way of working out." So Tiffany stayed.

Meanwhile, the youngsters were proving quite promising. What Knox and the Wilson sisters lacked in experience, they made up for with their winning attitude. They worked hard, listened, and loved to play. All their efforts had them on track to becoming players like Patricia Crowe.

Game two sent the Foxhounds back to Norfolk to play Old Dominion University (ODU). Before the team boarded the bus, Darren received an email from Jimmy.

"Hey Darren," the email read. "Sorry I can't make it tonight. I'll be paying attention though. And since I know you have been worrying about your team, I put together some ideas for you. Read it over and let me know your thoughts."

As the bus traveled back east on Interstate 64, Darren reviewed the remainder of the email:

Here are my thoughts on handling unhappy players. Good luck tonight. If you have any questions, see me, and I can clarify.

After a lifetime of dealing with unhappy players and employees, there are seven areas to consider when deciding how to address them.

The **first** is to determine if the player(s) have violated the standards and expectations. The **second** is the effect of this behavior on team dynamics. Synergy is the goal—great chemistry between teammates. **Third**, are you and your staff making an honest effort to mentor the players? Are you openly communicating? Are you helping improve the player's attitude? Are you doing your part? The **fourth** is evaluating the player's attitude and whether it impacts the team's on-court performance. You need to weigh the cost of losing the player against the benefits of keeping the negative influence. Is it addition by subtraction? The **fifth** thing to consider is how the player's attitude affects the other team members. Is it affecting the players negatively? The **sixth** area to consider is the player's personal development. Before you potentially dismiss anyone, ask yourself if you and your staff can provide support and guidance to grow and develop the total player. Lastly, the **seventh** area is about the player's overall attitude. Will they continue to work against the values and culture you are building? If so, it may be necessary to part ways. Creating and instituting a positive team culture is critical for long-term success.

Ultimately, your decision to remove a player is the last resort. We cannot save them all. As a leader, you must do everything possible to help your players improve and become team players.

I know you'll do what is best for everyone involved.—Jimmy

The tradition-rich Old Dominion Monarchs welcomed the VCSU Foxhounds for each team's second game.

The starting five did not include Tiffany Hitchcock. Darren could tell this exclusion upset her but instead kept his focus on the team and the task at hand. By the time he finally subbed her in, the game that had been tied at 8 quickly turned ODU's way at 18–8 within minutes. Darren called timeout.

Tiffany's body language screamed selfishness, and her play was uninspiring. Before Darren could speak, Crowe barked at the entire team, a fire burning in her eyes. "Let's go! We're better than this. We've worked our asses off this week. Guard your man, box out, screen, cut, and move without the ball. We can do it!" Crowe's fuse had burnt out. Darren did his best to read the room, remaining calm and confident in the huddle. He reinforced what Crowe said, and the nods from the other coaches showed they were in full agreement. The team broke the huddle to take the floor, responding with energy to Crowe's leadership.

VCSU played much better and finished the first half only four points down, 34–30. The second half was a mixture of both good and bad play. For a brief moment, the Foxhounds led 42–41 after a Knox putback. It was becoming apparent, as Jimmy had said during their synergy session, that the best five included Crowe, Peck, Knox, and the Wilson twins. The intensity was there each time they were on the court. Although they lacked experience, they compensated with a persistent desire to win. The difference was apparent when Davis, Slade, and Hitchcock played—Darren knew they still needed them. It would take time to mold this team.

After finding their fight in the second half, the game nonetheless ended with an ODU victory at 70–60. Crowe led the team with 25 points and 10 rebounds, and more importantly, with her attitude. She was stepping into that leadership role, constantly pushing her teammates and encouraging them when things went wrong. Crowe seemed to realize her role was more than just being the best player; she needed to be the leader and raise the level of her teammates by setting the example, remaining positive, and being more vocal. Crowe herself later said in the press conference, "I need to be better—we all need to play better. The coaches have prepared us. We just need to execute. Be consistent."

The Foxhound Five stepped up their game and spelled the starters twice with tremendous enthusiasm and effectiveness. The coaches took notice and commended them. The game had been close until it got away from the Foxhounds in the final few minutes. Even with two losses in the books, the program was clearly making gains.

In the locker room, Darren did his best to remain positive despite the defeat. He wasn't going to dress down everyone like the old Darren. He was slowly learning that was an unproductive tactic that did nothing but destroy morale. Instead, he focused on constructive criticism and pointed to several critical opportunities where a missed assignment, a failed box-out, or a turnover resulted in easy points for the other team.

"Ladies, use this loss as an opportunity to learn. You can learn quite a bit from failure if you use it properly." Darren paused to gauge the room, then continued. "We were doing some good things out there. A possession here or there makes the difference. We have to value each possession. I am proud of the effort. Foxhound Five, I am proud of you. You did a great job tonight. Things will turn. Just need to keep working. Stick with the process. We have a few days before the home opener, so keep your heads up. We will review the film, identify what we need to improve, and return to work. See you on the bus."

It was clear Darren himself was improving his post-game assessments and communication methods. Still, as he gathered his belongings, he remained concerned about his three upperclassmen. Darren knew he needed to play his younger team, who were buying into the program's philosophy. Two losses to start the season bothered him, even though he could see significant progress.

As they hit the road for their trip home, Darren pulled out his journal. He needed to analyze his own performance tonight, just as Jimmy always impressed upon him. Darren needed to see what he did well, what he could do better, and how he could do it. No waiting until later or another day, Darren needed to evaluate his performance when the details were still fresh and he was in the right frame of mind.

Jimmy had told Darren that week, "Coaches must prepare like players." It was an often repeated quote he adapted from his favorite Shakespeare line, "All the world's a stage and all the men and women merely players." It was a quick reminder that he was on a stage for everyone to see, even if he was on the sidelines. Darren needed to be "on" every day and every night.

Darren's post-game checklist read like this:

- ➲ Was I at my best?
- ➲ Did I let the team play?
- ➲ Did I teach effectively?
- ➲ Did I maintain a positive attitude?
- ➲ Did I remain poised when the game reached peak-intensity moments?
- ➲ Was I as prepared as I needed to be?
- ➲ Where can I improve, and how?

Before Darren closed his journal for the night, he wrote, *A leader was born tonight.*

25 STORIES

> *I never said anything to hurt anyone. What I said was meant to motivate, inspire, and educate potential athletes.*
>
> —Bill Russell,
> 11-Time NBA Champion

The VCSU campus had a newfound spark. There had not been this much excitement for women's basketball in years. The first two games were losses, but they were competitive losses. The future was now brighter than the present; the university had gotten incredible attention for its athletic surge, especially with Darren Blood heading up women's basketball. VCSU was front and center for this Saturday night contest. It was a miniature Flutie Effect.[2, 3, *]

Every day, the team was pushing through challenges. Giving praise was a daily exercise. Although the Foxhounds had not won a game, they were developing a winning attitude. The

---

* Known as the "Flutie Effect," this unintended consequence was first speculated in the years following Boston College quarterback Doug Flutie's infamous game-winning Hail Mary touchdown pass against powerhouse University of Miami in a nationally televised game. The Flutie Effect refers to increased publicity and distinction of an academic institution directly affected by the success of its football program, leading to significant increases in prospective student applications. According to articles published in *Marketing Science* and the *International Journal of Advertising*, the year following Boston College's win, applications to the school increased 30 percent.

routine of physically demanding practices, the early morning conditioning sessions, and the individual and team meetings were starting to make a difference. The campus community and Eagle Gap watched as the team's culture was built one day at a time.

✎ Darren ✎

Darren was shocked by the wave of excitement that hit him as he entered the Pic & Pac. It was game day in Eagle Gap. Instead of the usual hum of activity, it felt like an outright party. Nearly everyone in the place was wearing something VCSU—a hoodie, hat, or shirt—to show support. *You'd think the girls were playing for a league championship tonight, not Longwood University!* Darren thought. Still, Darren was pleased by the town's support, especially since it was his first time at the Pic & Pac with his entire coaching staff. He thought it was about the time his staff met Frankie and the many locals whom he chatted with most mornings. The excitement in the air nearly halted the staff in their tracks. Coach Alexander joked, "Can you imagine what will happen when we start winning around here? It'll be utter chaos!"

Pic & Pac regulars bombarded them with congratulations and engaged with the staff, talking basketball. It was evident that the campus and town were "all in" now. Darren felt proud that, by and large, the people of Eagle Gap and VCSU had noticed how he and his staff had stepped up. It made his long road back to coaching seem worth it, even if for a few minutes.

Word was also out about sophomore guard Patricia Crowe. Madie described her as "must-see TV," and Frankie and the Phanatics told Darren how much they loved that Crowe wore jersey number six because Madie's grandad was a massive

Celtics fan. Frankie was a Bill Russell fan too. Judging by sales made at the games, it was the hottest item in town.

🏀 🏀 🏀

In one of Darren's early meetings with Jimmy, he asked his old friend how he successfully motivated people. Jimmy's answer was simple: "Get them ready and in the correct frame of mind."

He continued, "I often tell stories that illustrate the message I wanted to deliver to the specified audience. It may be about overcoming adversity, teamwork, goal setting, leadership, etc. One thing to always remember when telling a story: Get the facts right. The date, the score, the people involved. Know the story."

"Where do you get these stories?"

"Books, YouTube, movies, documentaries, and articles— it's all at our fingertips. With a little research, you can find the perfect story to empower and galvanize your team," said Jimmy.

Darren reflected on this lesson all day as he gathered the team in the meeting room before the home opener. Crowe's number six had triggered a great story. The assistant coaches began by reviewing the opponent's strengths and weaknesses and how they would attack both areas. Then Darren took center stage with what he hoped would be a powerful story.

"On April 15th, 1965, the Boston Celtics and Philadelphia 76ers played game seven of the Eastern Conference Finals. Celtics center Bill Russell is considered by many experts as the greatest winner in sports history, with 11 NBA championships and 2 as a player-coach. With a 1-point lead, 110–109, the unthinkable happened. There were five seconds left to play, and Russell, who said he only trusted himself to make the inbounds pass, made a critical mistake. When he inbounded the ball, the ball hit a cable wire connected to the basket—Sixer's ball. Russell was distraught. He had carried the team for almost a decade, but in that moment, he begged someone to 'pick him up.' John Havlicek did just that, stealing the inbounds pass and saving the game; 10 days later, they won the NBA championship. So tonight, pick up your teammates when they make a mistake. Be leaders. Set the example. Play like champions."

Darren finished the story with energy, and the team sat in silence for a second. Then Crowe stood and brought the team together.

With all hands in, she said, "Tonight is our game. We play together. We play for one another. One mindset. One goal. There is no way we lose tonight. Believe it . . . 1-2-3, Hounds!"

The Crowe-led Foxhounds crossed the Green Line to loud cheers. Darren followed behind them and was glad to see the town's support. It felt like the team now belonged to something bigger than themselves.

The nearly sold-out Lewis Auditorium included two adversaries beyond the other team, Gene Hack and Dr. Kelly. Hack never passed on an opportunity to antagonize his professional rival, but Darren was glad to see Dr. Kelly in attendance.

Longwood University entered the game with one loss and one win—against Norfolk State, the same team that handled the Hounds just a few days ago. Still, Darren believed this was a winnable game. The starting five included Davis, Slade, and Hitchcock. It was a risk, one he'd discussed with the other coaches, but they finally agreed on the choice; it was a ploy to encourage the three upperclassmen. Failure to start the upperclassmen may have caused more harm than good.

From the tipoff, it was evident that the Foxhounds came to compete. Crowe hit three straight three-pointers, putting the Foxhounds up 9–0 within two minutes. For the rest of the first half, Darren only reacted when he gave the exiting players pats on the back. The Foxhound Five stormed the courts to spell the starters for three minutes. They ate the clock and took four quality shots, three of which hit nothing but net. Judging by cheers, the Foxhound Five were quickly becoming fan favorites.

The second quarter began with Crowe, Peck, Knox, and the Wilsons. The five played their hearts out. It was synergy at its finest. The three freshmen were tenacious on defense and hit the boards hard at both ends. The Foxhounds led 38–20 at halftime. It was not that close.

The second half was a carbon copy of the first. Crowe scored on the drive, on the break, and from the perimeter. She finished with 28 points. Peck controlled the offense without error, handing out 15 assists. Makayla Wilson got in on it too, setting an aggressive tone by diving after two loose balls. Knox had three blocks and out-rebounded everyone with a Bill Russell-like 20 rebounds. Darren was overcome with emotion as the horn sounded, signaling a 77–52 VCSU victory. It was his first win as a DI college head coach.

The post-game presser was a joyous one. Gene Hack was his usual self, seemingly trying to dampen Darren's joy. But Darren felt untouchable; even the buzzkill writer couldn't bring down his spirits.

"Coach, this is your first win in a long, long time. While that's all very impressive, how will you match up with other teams in the league, like Chattanooga and Wofford?" Hack's voice dripped with condescension. Chattanooga and Wofford were much better programs, and they both knew it. They were fresh off the court, and he was already downplaying the win. Darren was prepared.

"Well, Gene, I don't yet know," Darren responded. "It was a big win for our program tonight. We will enjoy this one and get back to work . . . tomorrow."

"Are you hoping to parlay this win and future successes into another shot at the NBA?"

Darren's inner thermostat started to rise. He took a sip of water to cool his temper and allowed himself to think, *That was a stupid question.* The old Darren might have said it aloud. But now he only coolly replied, "Gene, my only concern right now is establishing a winning attitude here." Although Darren was standing up to Gene, he could have sworn Dr. Kelly, who had been given access by Jimmy, smiled. She even grabbed a "We Want Blood!" T-shirt on the way out the door.

Moments later, Darren stood before the jubilant team and said, "That was an impressive display of teamwork. Coach Mays, Bennet, Moore, and Alexander, you did a tremendous job preparing the team. Ladies, you set the court on fire. Great job everyone." Darren didn't even need Jimmy's reminder to know this was a moment to praise the team.

🐾 Jimmy 🐾

As Jimmy walked down the hall from the press room, he could hear cheers from the locker room. He smiled at the nearby security guard and said, "These are the sounds we need to hear more of! It's called winning."

"Yes, sir," responded the guard with a smile.

However happy he was, though, Jimmy Harding knew that there would still be plenty of days when the struggle would feel unrelenting. The ups and downs of a season come as the sun rises and sets every day. The weeks ahead would be as challenging as those they had conquered. It was all part of transforming a losing program into a full-time winner.

MANAGING MOMENTS

> *If everyone is thinking alike, then someone isn't thinking.*
>
> —George S. Patton,
> United States Army General

✎ Darren ✎

It did not take long for the excitement from the home opening win to be diminished. VCSU split the next two games, followed by a disastrous performance in front of the home crowd against the University of Richmond. Gene Hack captured the brutal loss in his article, "Blood's Hounds Bitten by the Spiders." The first word in the article was "embarrassing," and the snide story continued as it described the 22-point home crowd loss. Hack refused to give any grace, even as he described Darren's post-game press conference. Darren had taken the blame for the loss, something he'd never done in the past, and yet the article called him pandering! The injustice had made Darren's teeth clench. He had to shake off the annoyance as he headed to meet Jimmy.

The mood at the Pic & Pac was sour. Darren and Jimmy arrived at the same time. In contrast to the gloomy atmosphere,

Jimmy seemed as cheerful as ever. Darren watched as he shook hands and made small talk before coming to join him in the back.

Before Jimmy could remove his coat, Madie slid two steaming hot coffees in front of them. "Here ya go."

"Thank you," Jimmy and Darren replied in unison.

"My pleasure," Madie said as she faded off to serve others.

"So, to business: We seem to have hit a wall. Jimmy, I know seasons have their ups and downs, but last night was a big step backward. We *stunk*. Tough to watch. It's been downhill since our home opener. What do you suggest we do to get this team going? I know what I used to do in these situations, but that didn't work out too well," Darren said.

Jimmy surprised him by smiling. "It was inevitable. Teams that are not used to winning—like us—have trouble dealing with success. Losing is easy. Consistently winning is hard. You handled it well. Better than NBA Coach Blood would have. Why don't you call Hack and tell him how much you've grown?!"

"Ugh. Hack. Don't get me started on him and his stupid article."

"Take heart, Darren. VCSU women's basketball is trending upward even with the loss. Don't panic. You are doing fine. The loss hurt, I'm sure, but it was a tremendous learning experience. Remember, it is winning and learning, not winning and losing. So take today's practice and follow the example of basketball coach Dean Smith of North Carolina. Smith gave his players a break from the grueling season playing volleyball instead of practicing basketball. It took their minds off of the game and gave them a chance to have fun and refresh. Then they could prepare for the conference and NCAA tournament."[4]

"You're joking."

"No, really," said Jimmy. "Try it today and see if you feel it was beneficial. If it doesn't work, we will MTA."

"Ok, it is worth a shot," said Darren. "Next question, who would you start?" Darren followed.

"I would switch up your starting five. Start Knox, Makayla, and Tiana Wilson with Crowe and Peck. Bring Ruby off the bench as a sixth man. As for Slade and Hitchcock, they can still help you, but not as starters. Foxhound Five. You've given them every chance to earn the job, and they have not earned it."

Darren, who had lost sleep over this, nodded in agreement.

"Now is the time," said Jimmy. "If not now, when?"

Darren could not disagree with his boss. At 2–4, it was as good a time as any to make a change to the starting five. Incorporating volleyball was new to him, but a lot of this was. He'd give it a try.

Jimmy added, "Darren, the job is about managing moments. The great coaches do it, and you are a great coach. I have no doubt you'll make it happen. One more thing—if I may."

"Of course Jimmy—I value your lessons."

"I also think you should let Crowe take charge a little more. She can score from anywhere. Get the ball in her hands as much as possible. She is a tremendous passer. That makes everyone better. From what I've seen, they feed off her energy. Make sure you give her that credit too. She is a power-four player. The former coach was lucky to get her, and we're even luckier that she stayed."

"She is a one-of-a-kind player, that's for sure."

"She reminds me of you a little bit, Darren."

Darren was surprised by the compliment. "Oh, thank you. But ego aside, she is better than I ever was. It's not even close. I'll turn her loose."

Later, Darren and his staff set up for the volleyball game. As the players jogged onto the court, he could see their surprise. They jumped into the game with enthusiasm, and Darren could tell the weight of the loss was soon lifted from everyone—even the coaches as they joined in the game. It was a day of smiles, positive talk, and improved body language. The storm clouds had lifted. As they wrapped up, Darren brought the team together.

"Great job today, ladies. I didn't realize we have a few volleyball studs on this team."

"Coach, I was all-district as a senior," chimed in Alicia Knox.

"Pipe down, rookie," said Vivian. Knox smiled.

Darren continued, "Let's understand we have to continue to work. Extra work early, stay late if needed. We have standards. Today was an opportunity to get our minds right. There is so much more out there for this team. Hey, you learn more from a loss than a win. Understand that. Learn from it. It is how you improve as a player and as a team. A lot of season left . . . Coaches, anything to add?"

Coach Mays kept it simple, "Great job today, ladies."

Coach Bennett, knowing player meetings were coming, reminded everyone to check their phones and emails for potential meetings that lie ahead. Many of the players nodded in agreement, but Darren noticed Tiffany looked nervous.

"1-2-3, Hounds!" They headed off the court.

Individual meetings in-season were on an as-needed basis. With the upcoming lineup changes, there was an immediate need. Darren's bedside manner in meetings was improving with help from Jimmy, who was a grandmaster in communication. Darren built on this advice, establishing some guidelines: All meetings would be confidential, designed to help the players, with an emphasis on putting the team first. Each player was evaluated as an individual, with no comparison between them. Darren repeated these guidelines as he prepped to meet his players.

Darren's job was to communicate changes to the starting lineup and let everyone know their role in the team's success. His coaching staff would sit in each of these meetings.

Ruby Davis was first. She entered Darren's office and promptly sat down, waiting for him to start the discussion.

"Ruby, we want to insert you as our sixth man. You're a versatile player who can score, rebound, and handle the ball. Hell, you can play all five positions if needed—that's skill. I believe the team would be better with you coming off the bench." Darren could see a little doubt in Ruby's eyes. "Have you ever heard of John Havlicek?" he asked.

"No, I haven't."

"Well, he was the sixth man on the legendary Boston Celtic teams of the 1960s. He revolutionized the position. His Hall of Fame coach, Red Auerbach, used to say, 'John was the guts of our team.'[5] I think you have that potential."

Ruby smiled at the praise as her mood turned from doubt to belief. "I trust you, coach. If you believe we can win with me in this role, I am good being our sixth man." She left with a nod. Darren hoped she could feel the trust they were putting in her and feel empowered by it.

Dominique Slade arrived shortly after Ruby left.

Darren squared his shoulders as he explained to Dominique that she would be taking a reduced role. She seemed to understand and even admitted that the new expectations were a more challenging adjustment than she thought. "I'm trying not to get discouraged, but it's been a major adjustment for me. I can improve though—it's just taking time."

Darren, recognizing her honesty, reassured her. "As a senior, it takes a lot of courage to admit that. And by accepting a reduced role, you will earn tremendous respect from your teammates. Trust me. We will be a better team with this move. And with your experience, the Foxhound Five will become a force to be reckoned with going forward. Just keep competing."

Dominique replied that she would. Darren was pleased with this positive outlook from her. *I needed that kind of win before meeting with Tiffany.*

Darren and his staff had determined this would be the toughest conversation of all. Although he was improving his empathy and listening skills, Darren needed to become a sports psychologist on the fly.

As Tiffany settled at the table, Darren began. "Tiffany, the coaches and I have made a decision to remove you as a starter. You will serve in a backup role on the Foxhound Five. Understand that you have made tremendous progress in many areas, but at this point, we believe you will be more productive for the team in this role. Plus, the Foxhound Five will drastically improve."

Tiffany, who was beginning to finally realize she was not behaving or playing at the expected level, quietly asked, "Where am I falling short? What do I need to work on?"

Those questions represented a different Tiffany Hitchcock. It was one willing to make the effort to change—or so it appeared.

"You are a lot like me," said Darren, pointing the finger at himself. "I hate when things are outside of my control. You could say I didn't handle it well. I punched a referee, remember?" Tiffany gave a small smile. "You are a good player, but you will be even better if you can focus on what you can control. This is where I would put my focus. You can only control your actions in the classroom, in meetings, at practice, and in games—not the situations themselves. Instead of sulking when things beyond your control are not in your favor, adapt and respond more positively. Learn to let things go. Here is an example. Let's say a ref makes a bad call. You can't control it, but you *can* control your response. When you respond poorly, your play suffers, and when your play suffers, the team suffers. We can improve this together. I am still learning. Dr. Harding has been working with me." Darren was showing more vulnerability. "Regardless of what you believe, I am here to help you with more than just basketball."

Coach Mays chimed in, "You will provide a spark for the team, something you can bring to the court in short bursts. No one else will have a player like you coming off the bench."

"And all of this could change very quickly," Darren said, "so you need to be ready to go."

Tiffany's attitude was unreadable, but she seemed to accept the news. As she left, Darren knew that only time would tell if she bought into the change.

With the three most challenging meetings over, Darren felt relieved. He was never quite comfortable with one-on-one meetings. The thought of demoting a young person or, even worse, suspending or dismissing them from the team weighed on him now, even though it never had before. But he was pleased with how the conversations went. It was decided: Ruby would be the sixth man, and Dom and Tiff would add experience to the Foxhound Five.

Just before the next pre-practice meeting, Darren and the coaches called Knox and the Wilson sisters to the office not long after Tiffany departed.

After telling the three freshmen of their promotion, each smiled and thanked the coaches.

Darren brushed away their thanks. "No, no. Thank you all for working as hard as you have. Great things are ahead for each of you. Trust me." He fist-bumped each before they headed out the door.

As the assistant coaches exited as well, Coach Mays said, "Now *that* is coaching right there. If you can keep that positive approach, this team will run with the big dogs, pun intended." Darren gave her an exasperated grin, but he was secretly pleased with the praise.

As Coach Mays and Darren walked to practice, he thought of the changes they were making. Some were conventional adjustments—would their new lineup make a difference? Some were unconventional—would adding volleyball as a change-of-pace, fun team-building exercise cure the hounds of their inconsistency? Two road games were creeping up soon. The so-called experts projected little chance of a win, but these setbacks could be a setup for a comeback. This was the approach the staff was taking. He was making the adjustments, and time would tell if they would move the team in the right direction.

27 IT'S THE LITTLE THINGS

> *The will to prepare to win is what is key,*
> *more so than the will to win.*
>
> —Bob Knight, Hall of Fame
> College Basketball Coach

🥊 Darren 🥊

After MTA and the introduction of the new lineup, the team's mindset exuded the confidence of a 6–0 team (despite its 2–4 record), a clear indication of their burgeoning self-belief. Complete buy-in was on the horizon.

Every practice had the same structure. They operated with a challenging and intense game-speed mentality. Darren and his coaches intentionally designed every drill to create competition. There was always a winner and a loser. Darren emphasized defense and becoming mentally quick. The defensive players were often disadvantaged, regardless of the drill: one-on-one, small groups, or team situations. Sometimes, the drill would be five-on-four or six-on-four to force the defense to work harder. Then there was his focus on mental quickness— switching the drill immediately. At any point during practice, the team would, for example, go from an offensive fast-break drill to a jump-shooting drill with pressure, or go from offense to defense. This developed the players' ability to think, adjust, and execute quickly and subconsciously for an immediate change—practicing at game-level intensity. Lastly and most importantly, each practice reinforced consistent coach-to-player, player-to-coach, and player-to-player communication. It was their foundation for progress.

As practice wound down, Darren strolled over to each staff member and quietly thanked them for their efforts. Weeks of praise and having the space to coach had noticeably increased their confidence.

Nearly 10 minutes before the end of practice, Darren blew the whistle. Everyone stopped. He said, "Ladies, that was an excellent practice. I have just one last thing on the agenda to make the practice even better. We need Jayla to make one free throw." Jayla Thorn was a junior Foxhound Five. She was a hard worker, and free throws were her thing. Darren felt confident about his chances of pulling off this team-building exercise. "The coaches and I have decided, if Jayla makes the foul shot, we shorten practice to 90 minutes tomorrow—if she doesn't, we do one set of what I call Sweet 16s. That's 16 touch-and-goes, sideline to sideline, in under one minute. And we'll put in our normal two-hour practice tomorrow."

"Great teams win by making clutch free throws late in the game," Coach Mays chimed in.

The team's enthusiasm and energy intensified. They clapped their hands, screamed, hooted, and cheered for Jayla in unison. Vivian grabbed a loose basketball and passed it to Jayla. "This is a hundred percent ball."

The noise slowly went silent as Jayla set her feet and bounced the ball. Before she crouched to shoot, Coach Mays blew the whistle and screamed, "Time out!"

The unexpected timeout added more pressure, but Jayla smiled and stepped away from the foul line to reset herself and get her mind right as the rest of the team whooped. "You got this," said Patricia Crowe.

Darren instructed the team to line up on the sideline. If Jayla missed, they would immediately start running. If she made it, they would go home winners.

The Lewis fell silent as Jayla crouched to shoot. The world seemed to stop. The ball soared from Jayla's hands with a perfect 12–6 rotation. The exuberant team sprinted to Jayla as the ball hit the bottom of the net. *Swish!* Tiffany and Makayla lifted Jayla onto their shoulders as they marched toward the Green Line. Practice was over. Darren looked on and smiled. He knew the team was more together than ever. The comeback was partially complete—Radford was next.

The blustery winter wind blew off the Blue Ridge Mountains into Eagle Gap. Winter in central Virginia had arrived with a fury. Southerners call it "scary cold." The Foxhounds, bundled in heavy coats, were dismayed to find that snow had crept its way to southwest Virginia. The cold weather was a complete 180 from inside Radford's Dedmon Center. Darren's ladies were anything *but* cold. They shot 55 percent from the floor, 40 percent from behind the three-point arc, and missed only one foul shot all night. The new lineup produced results. Davis was superb off the bench with 12 points, while Hitchcock and Slade gave the Foxhound Five a B-12 shot. Crowe and Peck were dominant, scoring 26 and 14, respectively. The three freshmen were complementary in every way. Strong on the boards and tenacious on defense. The 82–62 win was the best outing of the year—the most points scored by VCSU women since the Reagan administration!

The ride back to Eagle Gap was celebratory. While the players were immersed in the win, the coaches sat preparing for their next, biggest game yet. It was a hubbub of game review, self-scouting, scouring the opponent, and practice planning as the bus traveled north on the 18-wheeler-congested Interstate 81.

With UNC next, Darren knew his message to the team had to be perfect. He needed an inspired but relaxed team, and the biggest challenge was that *he* needed to be steady.

The cell phone rang. It was Jimmy calling.

"Hey, Coach. That was big. Big!" Before Darren could respond, Jimmy said, "Now it's time to stun the basketball world. VCSU beats Power Four and 25th-ranked North Carolina! How does that sound?"

Darren laughed, "That sounds pretty good. The team was as good as I've ever seen them. It was the least amount of coaching I've done."

"That should be a lesson right there. Be a great coach in practice, then let them play the game. Ranting and raving up and down the sidelines does not work like it used to. You've got this." Jimmy said goodbye, and Darren hung up, thinking.

North Carolina. Darren needed a great message—the perfect one to inspire great effort.

People were noticing the program now. Even Gene Hack had nothing to criticize. With one more win, VCSU would eclipse last year's three-win season. The catch? It was only the eighth game of the season. With nationally-ranked North Carolina next, Darren liked where his team was mentally, but he knew that change could happen in a few chaotic seconds. That moment could undo all of their hard work, and all coaches fear this happening.

Darren was busy talking to a group of students all decked out in VCSU gear as he waited for Jimmy to arrive at the Pic & Pac. Jimmy was on time, but Darren had gotten there extra early. He smiled at the president and soon joined him at their usual table.

"Grab a seat, Mr. Celebrity," Jimmy said, pushing the chair toward him. "You start winning around here, and who knows what may happen. Beat North Carolina at their home, and we may need to find a new meeting spot."

Before Darren could respond, Jimmy asked, "Have you ever heard of the 75–85 Principle?"

"Never."

"I learned it when I was a player at Georgia. My college coach used to remind us about the details and preparation needed to win, especially when the odds were stacked against us. That usually happened when we played Kentucky, Kansas, or Duke—times when we were the clear underdogs. Much like we are against UNC now."

Darren was intrigued and pulled out his journal to take notes as Jimmy continued. "Bear Bryant, the Hall of Fame football coach, told his Alabama team at the beginning of every year that they could win through daily preparation and attention to the details." Jimmy pulled out a piece of paper to better illustrate his point. "Bryant would say, 'Let's suppose the maximum ability of any player is 100.'" Jimmy wrote 100 on the paper. "'And you are a player with a 75 ability competing against another player with, let's say, an 85 ability.'" Jimmy wrote 75 on the left and 85 on the right. "'Now, because of your preparation and attention to the little things, you play a little above your head, perhaps at an 85 level.'" He crossed out the 75 and wrote 85. "'Then let's say your opponent did not pay attention to the little things—say one game they played below 85, even dropped off and played at a 75 ability.'" He crossed out the 85 and wrote 75. "Therefore, because of your preparation, attention to the little things, and giving a little extra, you can win."[6]

"I love it," Darren said. "I have been on both sides.

"I'm sure Carolina is going to take us lightly. I've seen it too many times. We need to be ready to take advantage."

Jimmy reminded Darren, "You can only control how you prepare, your attitude, and how you show up for practice and games. UNC could arrive ready to play above their ability or arrive under their 85. Control the controllable. Be ready at tip-off."

Darren grabbed his things and headed to the office. *I've got to teach this 75–85 Principle to the team.* Bear Bryant was one of the best ever, and this new principle was yet another clue of his success. Darren felt confident North Carolina would get 85 and even a little more from the Foxhounds.

DAVID VS. GOLIATH

> *Nothing is impossible with the right mindset.*
>
> —James "Buster" Douglas,
> Boxer and Heavyweight Champion

🏌 Darren 🏌

With little VCSU facing the nationally-ranked North Carolina Tar Heels, it was an early-in-the-season David versus Goliath meeting that the nation normally would pay little attention to. But Darren's courtside appearance made it must-see TV. The rampant publicity did nothing to alleviate the team's stress. Still, Darren knew his meeting about the 75–85 Principle had improved the team's mindset. The mood at the practices reached intensity levels that Navy Seals would have been proud of—Darren could barely believe this was the same program he'd inherited. He hoped the team's trust and sureness would carry into the UNC game and beyond.

As with the previous away games, VCSU made the trip south with the usual routine. All great coaches keep routines, whether on the road or at home, and now Darren was no exception. There were no surprises, nothing special. It was business as usual.

The day before the shootaround was intimidating, especially as the Foxhounds entered Carmichael Arena, the home of the Lady Tar Heels. The arena bore endless legacies of great players, most notably Michael Jordan, coached by the legendary Dean Smith. The place was dripping with history.

Darren watched as the team took in the space, awe on their faces. Patricia Crowe, in particular, seemed to appreciate the greatness of its history. She walked onto the court, gazing around. The energy of the arena seeped into the team, and Darren was impressed by their shootaround. At the end of practice, Patricia Crowe gathered the team in the center circle. Darren and the other coaches stood a step back, preparing for her pep talk to the team.

Patricia began, "Tomorrow night, we have a chance to shock the world." Darren nodded to the other coaches, confirming the team's leader was on the floor. He knew the impact the best player could have when they reinforced the coaches' principles, and Crowe was gearing up for a pep talk. She continued, "What better place to show the country that the Foxhounds are for real? These are the games we want to play in. The bigger the game, the better we play. I want everyone to be at full speed, locked in. Don't worry about mistakes. I got you. Get your mind right! Start seeing it now! We've done the work—we've paid the price and done the little things. We're prepared. Now it's time to show them us Foxhounds are here to fight."

The team nodded in agreement and put their hands in: "1-2-3, Hounds!"

Game day. Darren's loud, excessive pre-game speeches used to be his ammunition. That cringe-worthy, R-rated language was not acceptable today. His over-the-top performance had briefly worked in the NBA, but over time, those words and his temper had lost all effectiveness.

Darren watched the team try to relax before they took the floor. Crowe made the rounds to see and speak with each player. She was the glue. The room became quiet.

Darren spoke with confidence to the team, "You are ready. You have prepared. Our coaches have done an outstanding job getting us to this point. Now it's your time. Play with great energy, enthusiasm, and excitement. Control what you can control. Be leaders! Be a great teammate, pick each other up, and do your job. Accept the challenge you have and enjoy it. I cannot wait to watch you tonight." With that last bit of encouragement, the team jogged out onto the court while the coaches settled courtside.

The Tar Heels were led by UNC preseason All-American guard Gabby Reynolds and preseason all-conference center Devon Blue. Darren knew these two would be problems for the Foxhounds. He could only hope they would play under their 85 ability.

VCSU won the tip. Peck hit Crowe, who cut through the UNC defense and made a no-look pass to Mikayla Wilson, who was primed and ready for a short jumper off the glass, quickly giving them a 2–0 lead. After several possessions and missed shots by the Tar Heels, Peck, not known to score, hit two three-pointers as VCSU quickly built a 14–2 lead before UNC called a timeout. The crowd was visibly stunned.

"Hey, is this fun or what?" Darren asked, his face lit with joy. "Tiffany, Dom, and Rube, let's go." The demoted upperclassmen were in. Coach Mays sidled up to him and asked why he took out the freshman—not to challenge the decision, but out of genuine interest. Darren shared his strategy, "We will need experience at some point, so I wanted to get them in as soon as possible. Get them in the flow of the game. Plus, it's three fresh bodies. Blue is a handful. We need to keep a fresh player on her all night. Make it as tough as possible." Coach Mays nodded her understanding, and they sat watching the game unfold.

Crowe and Peck continued to dominate. The entire arena was stunned. Dribbling, passing, and attacking the rim created easy shots for Knox and the twins. The half ended with VCSU ahead 36–29. In Eagle Gap, the excitement grew as the possibility of a major upset was only 20 minutes away.

At the half, Darren turned the team over to his assistants to make the adjustments. He was still coming to grips with delegating; as a micro-manager in the NBA, he now took the advice of his mentor to let the others coach. Courtside, Jimmy's words echoed in his ears: "Even though you think you know more—and you may—your coaches are good too. They should be an extension of you. The players won't think less of you if you sit back and listen to the others—everyone will respect you more. If you relinquish control, you will gain it."

Carolina began to flex its muscles in the second half, and Reynolds started to show exactly why she was destined to play at the professional level. Blue and company began to dominate the boards. UNC led 49–48 at the end of the third quarter.

Darren asked his team in the huddle, "If I told you we would have 10 minutes to play and were down by one, what would you say? Would you take it?"

The consensus was, "Of course."

Crowe spoke up. "We've played our asses off here tonight. We have 10 more minutes. Let's go!" she barked as she threw her towel to the floor. The team broke the huddle with Crowe,

Peck, Knox, Davis, and Makayla Wilson (the better scorer of the two Wilsons).

The crowd was anything but relaxed as the underdog Foxhounds refused to be intimidated. With VCSU down two at 61–59 and less than 90 seconds remaining, the game turned. Peck drove the lane hard and scored but collided with Gabby Reynolds, who was late helping on defense. The whistle blew. The official signaled the charge. No basket. And that's when it happened.

Darren's careful control collapsed.

He exploded off the bench in a rage with a horde of expletives. "That's a f****** block! That's bull shit. Not close! Are you f****** kidding me!" UNC knew it, the crowd knew it, and the game announcers knew it. Everybody watching knew it. Peck was visibly devastated. Darren was furious. He was *steaming*. He'd lost all control. Coach Alexander did his best to keep a hold on Darren, preventing him from getting too close to the referee, who immediately called the technical foul. UNC was awarded two shots and the ball. With the score 63–59, VCSU was forced to foul. Two UNC free throws made it 65–59. Crowe missed a three-pointer, followed by a foul. UNC added two more free throws. The final score was North Carolina 67, VCSU 59.

In the face of defeat, Darren still could not get a grip on himself. He continued to bark at the official as he exited the court. He knew his reaction had cost his team a potential well-earned win, one that could have meant everything for the program. As Darren disappeared under the seats, he found an empty hallway out of sight. He stopped and leaned against the wall. Coach Alexander remained with him, just in case. Darren's thoughts ranged from still-burning rage to a sick feeling of shame that made him want to vomit. Neither coach spoke.

29 RESOLVE

> *Fall seven, rise eight.*
>
> —Japanese Proverb

⚔ Darren ⚔

The loss was crushing, and while admitting fault would've been unfathomable for the previous Darren, this time, he took the blame. It wasn't easy to do; despite Jimmy working to show him otherwise, admitting fault still felt like a sign of weakness to Darren, not strength. The team, however, felt very differently. They accepted the coach's apology, appreciated his openness to admit it, and loved that he had their backs. As much as the defeat hurt, the team was galvanized by their close loss against a team that no one believed they could challenge at all. Sure, they lost, but they managed to hold their own on the court with one of the best schools in the nation. Even though there are no moral victories, this was really a victory in and of itself.

Before boarding the bus home from Chapel Hill, Darren received a text from Jimmy: *"It happens, Darren. Don't beat yourself up. You've been doing a great job, and the team played well. I'm proud of you. See you Monday at 7:31 a.m."* Darren smiled a little at his phone as he read it. It was exactly what he needed to hear in a bad time, and the silent ride home was now almost bearable.

That Monday at 7:31 a.m., Darren walked into the Pic & Pac, not knowing what to expect. Frankie was the first to greet him. "Coach, that was a tough one. But the girls gave 'em hell!" Darren started to explain his mistake, but Frankie cut him off. "Don't matter about that technical. A coach has to do what a coach has to do, and the ref missed the damn call anyway." Darren felt appreciated during one of the lower points of the season.

Jimmy arrived and got right to the point. "Fall seven, rise eight . . . fall seven, rise eight. That's the message. When you get knocked on your ass, you have to get up off the mat. Here is your chance to do it, especially after coming so close. They put up a valiant effort, and they did it under your leadership. I won't pretend that I'm not disappointed by your . . . *response* to the bad call, but I want you to focus on all the positives and move forward."

"You always have a good message for me, boss. Thank you," Darren said.

"Listen, you know you reacted poorly—at least I hope so," Jimmy said.

"I do."

"Good. And now we can put that behind us and get to the lesson." Jimmy shifted gears. "You've made the commitment to be consistent—the results speak for themselves—but let's take it a bit further. Focus on getting better each day. The Japanese call it kaizen: continuous improvement in small increments. It runs parallel with the 'one percent better every day' catchphrase."

Darren had his journal out and was making notes as Jimmy spoke.

"You have been unknowingly pursuing kaizen since day one, but let's make it intentional now. Make those improvements, however small, and don't settle for the status quo. Address problems as they arise. You're proof that kaizen can work over time. You've improved control of your emotions. You empower your assistants. And your communication skills? Utterly recognizable compared to how you started the season. If you had these skills years ago, you'd still be in the NBA winning championships."

"You're not wrong, Jimmy. That seems like a lifetime ago. But I think I needed to hit rock bottom. Reconnect with you. Work with these ladies. It's been life-changing. I'll forever be thankful."

"No thanks needed. I just knew you were the right fit." Jimmy smiled at him. "I've got one more thing on the agenda: a new coach's show. We'll kick off our first morning show on the second Monday after the New Year and run the show through the rest of the season. With our growing fan base, I'm sure it'll be a hit."

Darren's mood instantly changed. Jimmy's belief in him once again proved why leadership is essential. In one of his toughest moments, his leader wasn't trying to kick him while he was down; he was thinking of ways to improve the program, all while supporting his coach, regardless of his faults.

"I'll keep you posted as we get closer. Our play-by-play guy, Rick Haney, will host the show," Jimmy said.

"He's good," Jimmy said, and he meant it. Haney was young, but he was quickly becoming a local legend. He'd served as the voice of high school sports in central Virginia for the last decade and had amassed a significant social media following in that time. Haney's local fame and online platform were two big advantages that made Harding choose him, as he was looking to make a splash with a fan favorite. Beyond that, Jimmy was notorious for finding good people who had earned an opportunity to advance in their chosen field. It was one of the reasons why everyone loved him. He gave opportunities to those who were otherwise overlooked. And those who were given those opportunities were grateful and worked hard to pay Jimmy back. Just like Darren.

As the meeting between Darren and Jimmy concluded, they departed to their regular daily routine. Darren's routine offered no surprises. It always came with intention. Today's routine, though, came with a small twist: a catered dinner after practice. Again, an intentional diversion. After a tough loss, it was Jimmy's way to thank everyone. "Always reward effort and display loyalty," he would say. This dinner was a message to the team: *We see all that you are doing. Thank you. Keep it going.*

At the dinner table, there was a note for each player, personally thanking each and every one of them for their efforts and improvement this season. It included a famous Japanese proverb—one the girls had probably heard plenty of times by this point.

Fall seven, rise eight.

Your Biggest Fan,

Dr. Jimmy Harding

As Patricia Crowe read it, she turned to Peck and said, "Harding really is amazing. He's got a way of making people want to follow him anywhere."

Darren smiled as he saw another Jimmy lesson in effect: By treating the players the way they wanted to be treated, Jimmy could get more from his people than leaders who do the opposite.

30

MTA

> *Stay committed to your decisions, but stay flexible in your approach. It's the end you're after.*
>
> —Tony Robbins,
> Motivational Speaker

✎ Darren ✐

The pain was obvious to everyone watching the disastrous scene. Vivian Peck lay face down, holding her ankle with one hand and making a fist with the other. She was down, and she was not getting up. The practice floor became deathly silent as the girls stopped playing and gathered around.

The younger Darren Blood would have stepped over the injured player, looking for their replacement and trying to remove the damaged goods immediately so the practice could continue on. The old Coach Blood was heartless—an old-school mindset. Today, Darren's mindset had come full circle. He was concerned and displayed compassion, especially since he'd experienced his share of ankle injuries. The team saw it.

Next to Crowe, Peck was second in command, an extension of the head coach on the floor. As the point guard, she was equivalent to a quarterback. The timing of this injury could not have been worse—and everyone knew it. As the trainers worked on Vivian, the coaches briefly conversed. Crowe took the reins and brought the team together. At her command, the team split into four small groups to shoot foul shots at the portable practice baskets stationed along the main court sidelines. They did it without one word from the coaches, but Darren was not surprised by the team's resolve to finish the practice. Crowe, once again, displayed fantastic leadership.

"Tough day, ladies," Darren said at the end of practice. "I appreciate you finishing up strong. Unofficially, Vivian appears to be out indefinitely. But let's not worry about what we can't control. We will adjust." The team was shaken but still had faith in the coach. Darren could tell that they believed him when he said they would be okay.

When the ladies exited the floor for the locker room, Darren stepped aside and sent Jimmy a short text: "*Bad news, boss. Vivian injured her ankle. Talk tomorrow, 7:31 a.m.*" Jimmy immediately called to ask, "How bad is the injury?"

"They told me it's a grade-two sprain—four to six weeks. A big blow to our team."

"Well, we can't do anything about that. The only thing you can control is the choices you make now. We will discuss it further tomorrow morning. Don't let it get you down too much."

Darren did his best not to fret. He asked his assistants to brainstorm some potential adjustments to discuss together. Then, he spent the rest of the night reflecting on how far the team had come and how to make the adjustment.

Jimmy did not waste time when he sat down across from Darren at the Pic & Pac. "I am sure you and your staff have thought of a few solutions to the problem, but before you tell me what you're thinking, let me tell you a story."

"In 1975, the Cincinnati Reds were 12–12 and needed a spark. Pete Rose was their left fielder. Rose had played left field for eight years—a Gold Glover in 1969 and 1970. They wanted to insert a young George Foster to play left field and add some punch to the feeble Reds' offense. So, manager Sparky Anderson went to Rose and asked if he could move to third base to get Foster in the lineup as the left fielder. Rose, the ultimate team player, only asked, 'When' Sparky wanted to make the change on Friday. It was a Tuesday. Rose had three days to prepare. A man who played eight years in the outfield would change positions mid-week. Well, it worked. Those Reds with Rose at third base went 96–42 the remainder of the season, and the Big Red Machine was born. They would win the '75 World Series and sweep the Yankees in the 1976 World Series."[7]

Darren asked Jimmy, "What would you do?"

"I would go to Patricia Crowe and ask her to move to point guard. Move Ruby Davis into the two. She has the skills. There's your best five: Crowe, Davis, Knoxy, and the Wilsons."

Darren was thinking the same thing but had taken a lesson from his boss—asking what Jimmy thought, then giving him all the credit for the idea. Jimmy told him later that this was when he realized Darren was finally getting this people skills thing going.

Darren sent Crowe a text to come to the office early. The staff loved the idea of moving Crowe. But the most important person had yet to be asked.

"I played point guard my whole life until my junior year in high school," said Crowe. "That's no problem—no problem at all." Crowe's confidence was undisguised. Darren and his team never had a doubt she would think of the team first. In less than a day, their outlook did a full 180. Crowe was the Foxhounds' Pete Rose.

HISTORY AND WINNING UGLY

31

> *A generation which ignores history has no past and no future.*
>
> —Robert Heinlein,
> Science Fiction Author and
> Aeronautical Engineer

✍ Darren ✍

"Get there early, and don't worry about basketball for a day," Jimmy said. "Always take advantage of the opportunity to teach, no matter the subject, and there is no better place to learn about our nation's history than in our nation's capital. And we both see it—these kids don't know anything about history. They think the Dust Bowl is a football game on New Year's Day." Darren was skeptical about leaving early and taking focus away from preparing, but Jimmy insisted. "Trust me, Darren. The girls need a little culture, and so do you. You're prepared. You've done the work. Go enjoy what DC has to offer."

With the capital streets adorned with holiday lights, bows, and wreaths, there was no mistake about the most festive time of year. The VCSU Foxhounds arrived at dusk, thinking of the day after next when they would take on George Washington University and then battle the suburban counterpart, American

University, less than 24 hours later. For the moment, though, the team had a day to explore DC and enjoy themselves before preparing for the back-to-back games.

The nation's capital offered an abundance of history. An early morning walking tour was scheduled on the National Mall, where Dr. Martin Luther King Jr. stood to deliver his "I Have a Dream" speech. This left a significant impact on several players. The team finished the day with a tour of Ford's Theater. The majority of the players had never heard the name John Wilkes Booth, much less what he did to our country in 1865. It was a great history lesson.

As Darren walked the mall grounds, he reflected less on his past troubles and more on the opportunity he had been given. An introvert away from the court and locker room, Darren could see the value in these little things Jimmy was providing. Win or lose, this trip would be a success in its own right. The players may not recognize the value of the journey, but they will understand more as they grow older. Darren told Coach Alexander, "My parents grow wiser with each and every day."

The games arrived with great anticipation. The butterflies in Darren's stomach fluttered just before tipoff—that sick feeling of not knowing what could or may happen without their floor leader. Seconds after the tip, Darren's stomach settled as it was clear the Foxhounds would not miss a beat with Crowe at the point. Playing at breakneck speed, Crowe took charge, running the floor and the team with a gunslinger's swagger. It was a no-contest from the start. Even the Foxhound Five, which had to adjust because of Peck's absence, played flawlessly with the extended court time. The halftime speech lasted all of 30 seconds. VCSU led by 20. *"Just keep the pressure on them,"* was Darren's message. Simple is always better than complicated.

As the team exited the huddle to start the final 20 minutes, Crowe said, "Let's blow these mother you-know-whats off the court." And they did. The 77–58 win was the most convincing VCSU had seen in a long time.

Jimmy's text message read, "*Great win. It will mean even more if you play well in the next game.*" Darren thought to himself how true that was. Jimmy quickly followed up with, "*My advice—say little. It'll get you more.*"

Day two was different. The second-day game came a little earlier since VCSU and American were the visiting teams. The Foxhounds were now 4–5, one win more than the entire season a year before. Confidence was building—the type of confidence a good coach does not fiddle with. The coaches were smart; they let them play.

When Jimmy took on the task of transforming the basketball program, he knew there were things he could control. Unbeknownst to anyone other than Jimmy, the three-day DC excursion was part of the overall plan. A road trip with games on back-to-back days was difficult and tournament-like. And to win a tournament, a team must play on back-to-back days to hoist a trophy. It was a smart strategy few realized. He often said, "Achievement is never accidental, and those who think it is are fools."

Darren viewed this game as a potential tipping point to the season. With the all-important conference season ahead, American University became the perfect opponent. American was more David than Goliath. In Darren's mind, this was a must-win game. He had to fight his past to ensure he didn't place any undue pressure on the team. He couldn't spoil the energy the team was creating after Peck's injury. He did his best to be positive.

Before, Darren's message to his NBA guys on so-called must-win games was mixed with both positive and negative comments. His zest for perfection often led to overcoaching. His tone and message frequently sucked the life out of the collective. One former Knicks player said after Darren was dismissed, "Before games, he was guitar-string tight. He was never relaxed, so we were never relaxed. During games, you could never get comfortable playing. He'd be cursing your ass during the game. It was miserable playing for him."

Although Darren felt nauseous with pent-up anxieties, he did his best to look Pat Riley-cool so his team would not catch on. He smiled and walked tall in a comportment of confidence, even if his lunch threatened to make a comeback. Darren was emotionally different than in the previous games. It was that win-at-all-costs sensation he hoped to avoid.

The Crowe-led Foxhounds were too much for the lesser-talented opponent. The low-post advantages, including the Wilson twins' and Knox's size and athleticism, proved overpowering for the smaller American University Eagles. Even Hitchcock and Slade, who played backup roles, were effective—attitudes aside. The 61–44 win was unattractive, even downright ugly. For the first time as VCSU's head coach, Darren fought his nature to rip the team for its ineffectiveness and what he believed was uninspired play. He kept his composure on the sidelines throughout the game, but his core temperature rose.

As Darren walked to the locker room after shaking hands with the opposing coaches and players, his assistant coaches sensed his disapproval.

"Winning when you play poorly is a good sign," Coach Mays said. "Think of the doubt and uncertainty we had coming here."

"We exceeded expectations," Coach Morris said.

"We did what many others thought could not be done," Coach Bennet said.

"That was a big road win, Coach. To come on the road without our point guard and win two is big," Coach Alexander added.

Darren grinned. With his hands on his hips and head tilted back, Darren took a deep breath and exhaled. "You're right, you're right. Let me get my thoughts together here for a sec," Darren said as he walked in a small circle, gathering his composure. The assistants looked at one another, each envisioning what it must have been like after bad losses and ugly wins in those NBA locker rooms.

For the first time ever, Darren was aware of his emotional state. Feelings of anger, rage, and irritation bubbled to the surface. He noticed it. It scared him. *Where did this come from, and why?* he asked himself. With help from his well-aware assistant coaches, he breathed deeply and gathered himself.

At the doorway to the loud locker room, Darren paused to reboot. Once in the locker room, he immediately realized the damage he would have caused had he brought his lousy attitude and infected what was now a confident and excited team. If he had been one bit negative, it could have erased all the good gained over these last couple of days.

Crowe was making the rounds, high-fiving, fist-pumping, and hugging her teammates. Even Vivian Peck, in her walking boot, was congratulating her teammates. The smiles on their faces and the euphoria showed Darren what this program had been missing for over a decade: a feeling that they could accomplish something.

Darren kept it brief. "That was a gutsy performance today. As Coach Mays told me right after the game, it is a good sign when you win while not at your best. Great job by everyone." If only they had seen their coach minutes before he entered.

The Foxhounds left DC at 5–5—and a little more educated on US history. Not five minutes into the trip home, a text arrived from Jimmy. "*Way to go Darren! I know we didn't play well. That alone will keep you focused and fueled. Enjoy the win and the ride home, Jimmy.*"

The conference season had arrived. The coach's poll pegged VCSU for last place. In their minds, little had changed up there in Eagle Gap. It was Groundhog Day in the Southern Conference.

SUMMARY OF PART III:
THE SEASON BEGINS

1. **Build Daily Routines**

   This creates consistency and reduces surprises. Establishing routines allows teams to know what to expect each day, reducing stress and uncertainty. Consistent actions build habits that drive behaviors, producing the results we want.

2. **Create Synergy**

   The total is greater than the sum of its parts. Success isn't just about having talented individuals; it's about how well they work together. A cohesive team can achieve more when its members collaborate effectively. In basketball, play your best five, not your five best.

3. **Use Storytelling as a Leadership Tool**

   People connect with and remember a well-told story. Stories are powerful because they engage emotions, teach lessons, and make experiences more memorable.

4. **Manage Moments**

   Great leaders stay calm and avoid knee-jerk reactions. Leaders who react on impulse can cause more harm than good. Stay composed and help your team navigate challenges more effectively. Set the example on how to handle adversity—your team will follow.

5. Celebrate the Small Wins

By celebrating small wins, your people will feel good. It will motivate them to continue to improve, and most importantly, it improves the morale of the team.

6. Make Everything Count

Small details matter in achieving success. Whether it's preparation, execution, or reflection, every aspect contributes to the final outcome. Successful leaders and coaches focus on the "little things." Small things lead to greater things.

7. Seek to Compete Against the Best

To separate yourself, your team, or your organization, choose hard over easy—every time. The most valuable lessons often come from tackling the most difficult tasks.

8. Make the Adjustments

Adjust your strategies as needed. Be adaptable. When things don't go as planned, successful leaders are flexible. They make necessary adjustments and keep moving forward. Always focus on what's within your control—your attitude, effort, and actions.

9. Lifelong Leaders are Lifelong Learners

Leaders are teachers who share knowledge. True leaders are not just authority figures; they are mentors. By teaching others, leaders create a legacy of growth and development. Make every situation a teaching moment.

PART III
REFERENCES

1. Angela Duckworth, *Grit: The Power of Passion and Perseverance* (Scribner, 2018).

2. Doug J. Chung, "The Dynamic Advertising Effect of Collegiate Athletics," *Marketing Science* 32, no. 5 (2013): 679–698, https://doi.org/10.1287/mksc.2013.0795.

3. Charles R. Taylor, "How Much Does an NCAA Basketball Championship Matter: A Call for Research on the Public Relations Impact of Athletic Success," *International Journal of Advertising* 35, no. 4 (2016): 617–621, https://doi.org/10.1080/02650487.2016.1179856.

4. Dean Smith, Gerald D. Bell, and John Kilgo, *The Carolina Way: Leadership Lessons from a Life in Coaching* (Penguin Books, 2005).

5. "NBA's Best Sixth Men," *Sports Illustrated*, December 7, 2007, https://www.si.com/nba/2007/12/07/07-0nbas-best-sixth-men.

6. "Bear Bryant Locker Room Speech to Incoming Freshman," posted August 2, 2010, YouTube, 2 min., 17 sec., https://youtu.be/WVzETb9FSMw?si=9A9AzwOrV9dZ8rvN.

7. Rory Costello, "1975 Reds: Pete Rose Mans the Hot Corner," Society for American Baseball Research, accessed February 20, 2025, https://sabr.org/journal/article/1975-reds-pete-rose-mans-the-hot-corner/.

PART IV
CONFERENCE SEASON

32 | WINNERS NEVER QUIT

> *Quitting is not an option. I will not let anyone on this team quit.*
>
> —Herm Edwards,
> Former NFL Player and Coach

Darren

Tiffany Hitchcock was at it again. AWOL. The team and coaches worried, and practice went by at a difficult, unproductive pace. Tiffany had been a distraction before, but only days before the team was to open conference play, her timing could not have been worse.

As Darren walked toward his glass-cased office, he found Tiffany Hitchcock sitting on the floor at the foot of the door, her head down. A cold trickle of anxiety went down his stomach as he spotted her. Tiffany had had her troubles, but in the eyes of the coaches, she was still an important player. Even if she wasn't, she was still a young person in need of guidance. This situation was yet another test for the head coach, who, by all measures, was learning how to deal with people better each day.

As Darren moved closer, Tiffany rose to her feet. When she met Darren's gaze, he noticed her bloodshot eyes and red cheeks. This was a girl in distress, and Darren knew that it was more than just basketball. He thought of Jimmy's lesson: "Whenever you need to discuss difficult situations with a player, staff member, or anyone with a conflict, the office can corner the person. Get out and walk around campus. The walk can often eliminate the tension, making conversation easier." Darren gave it a shot.

"Hey, Tiff, let's go for a walk," he said.

The cold January air hit them square in the face as they exited the doors. They walked without speaking. Darren waited until they had gone some distance and then asked, "So what's going on?" He tried to keep his voice as neutral and open as he could.

"Coach, I don't think I want to play anymore," Tiffany said. "It's not working."

"Really? Why? You've been doing great," Darren said, shocked by her sudden declaration. "You're a senior, we're playing well, and you're a big part of that. What makes you want to quit now?"

She hesitated. Then, she stopped walking.

With her head down, she said, "I'm a senior, and I'm not even starting anymore. My dad is pretty hard on me. I've never lived up to his standards." Her voice came out quiet, choked with despair. "He played college basketball too. He had been an amazing player, a history-making type, and expects me to be just like him. But I'm not."

"Wouldn't he be upset, mad, disappointed if you quit the team?" Darren asked. "Wouldn't this make it even worse?"

Tiff didn't answer, instead saying, "I feel like such a loser. My grades suck. I don't start. I came in expecting to win and get better—all we've done is lose. It's frustrating."

Darren waited a few seconds. "Wouldn't he be more upset if you quit than if you continued to play?"

"I don't know . . . maybe, probably," Tiffany answered.

As they continued to walk, they came upon the university coffee shop. "Let's grab a cup of coffee," Darren suggested. "I'm a little chilly. What do you want, Tiff? It's on me. Latte, cappuccino, whatever you want."

Coffee in hand, Tiffany started to relax a little. They sat, and Darren shifted the discussion. "Have you ever heard of Joe Greene? Mean Joe Greene?"

"Never. His name was Mean Joe?"

"Yeah. Well, Mean Joe was a star defensive lineman for the Pittsburgh Steelers. Joe was a great player and an emotional player. As his name implies, he was one of the toughest and meanest players in the NFL. After a bad loss in 1974, Joe decided he wanted to quit. He'd had enough, and so he went home and stewed. The first day back, he went to his locker and grabbed his things. As he took those steps out of the building, he thought, 'Somebody, please stop me.' An assistant coach, Lionel Taylor, saw him walking out and said, 'Hold up a minute.' They sat in Joe's car and talked. Joe decided to go back, and you know what happened, Tiff?"

"No, what?"

"The Pittsburgh Steelers won their first Super Bowl that year, beating the Minnesota Vikings 16–6. Joe even had an interception in the game. The Steelers won three more Super Bowls in the next five years, and Joe Greene was elected into the Hall of Fame after he retired. Now, imagine if Joe would have quit in 1974. There may have been no Super Bowl victories or Hall of Fame."[1]

Tiffany sat quietly, sipping her hot latte, letting the story of Mean Joe sink in.

"Look at me, Tiff," Darren said. She turned.

He looked into her eyes and said, "This is your senior year, and while you may not think so, you have made tremendous strides. You've done wonderful work, and I appreciate your efforts and acceptance of your role. It takes a big person to accept what you and some of your teammates have. And trust me, quitting is never the answer."

"I wanted to be a WNBA player. But now, I don't know exactly. Maybe work in the WNBA or sports in some way. I do love basketball. It has been my whole life, but it hasn't worked out. Is that stupid?" Tiffany asked.

"No, it's not stupid. It's great to have goals. You must have goals, and I probably should have asked you what yours were from the start. That's on me. I'm sorry. But, no way, it's not stupid. It's great you have a goal. Quitting is the easy way out. We have been teaching the team to understand that all great things are accomplished after a difficult path."

They sat for a minute as they watched the coffee shop suddenly fill with students coming in for their midday caffeine fix. Then, the conversation turned to the team. Tiffany was coming around feeling a little more comfortable.

"Can I come back to practice tomorrow and be with the team?" she asked.

"Absolutely."

As the conversation continued, a small group of students walked up to say hello to Tiffany. She didn't know them, but they recognized her. At 6'4", she was a dead giveaway. They congratulated her on the team's success.

One asked, "Is this the famous NBA coach?"

"Yeah," Tiffany said, a small smile growing as she spoke. "He's the one."

"Cool. I thought so."

The other asked, "Aren't you one of the centers? Hitchcock, right?"

"Yeah, that's me."

"Can we get a photo with you guys?"

The group of six squeezed together. As the group walked off, wishing luck to both, Darren turned to Tiffany and asked, "Do you want to give all of this up?"

She just put her head down and unassumingly said, "No, not really."

Now that the fire with Tiffany had been doused for the time being, all of the attention turned to the Mercer Bears, who were coming to town for the all-important conference home opener.

While The Lewis was not sold out, there was a palpable excitement for the conference home opener. The two ticket booths resembled the opening night of a summer blockbuster, with long lines wrapping around the building. Inside, the noise grew—the band, the cheerleaders, the crowd. It was intoxicating.

From the tip, the Foxhounds played tight. Mercer controlled the first five-plus minutes, pulling out to a 12–0 lead. Most coaches would have called for a timeout, but Darren kept his poise and waited for the first media timeout. The auditorium was silenced. The crowd was dazed and confused and took the standing eight count. Darren had seen this more times than he cared for in New York.

In those days, an expletive-laced, spit-flying, one-way discussion would follow the timeout. One former player said, "There were some words I ain't never heard of, and I thought I had heard 'em all. I don't miss those timeouts." As much as it pained him, Darren kept his poise and tried something he'd never thought he would do. With a group of ladies about to come unglued, Darren said, "Isn't this great?" They all looked at him as if he was an unmedicated psychopath.

"Look, we are fine. Relax, deep breath. We're okay," said the unruffled head coach. "We had to give them some momentum." Darren then turned to Patricia Crowe, who was looking right back at him. "Trish, just settle down on offense. We are trying to create something when there is nothing. We are forcing it. Slow down and control the tempo. We control it. Not them." Crowe nodded in agreement. "Tiffany, you are in for Makayla." This was more for Tiffany's confidence than Makayla's play. Darren's social awareness at this critical moment was spot on with his most troubled player.

"Look over there—they are overconfident," Darren added comedically. The team smiled at this, some almost letting out a belly laugh. "Lotta game left."

Each assistant looked at one another, astounded at what they had just witnessed. Coach Bennet quietly said, "That was great coaching." They all sat and waited to see how that composed, inspiring talk affected the team.

The Foxhounds took the floor, more relaxed. Crowe did what she was told and took her time to find her groove penetrating, dissecting, and dishing to the VCSU version of the Twin Towers—Knox and Hitchcock.[2] At 6'4", both matched up physically with most teams. Mercer struggled to handle both. It was easy buckets for the tall tandem. *This lineup is tough to handle*, Darren thought with pride.

The crowd found its second wind when Crowe ended the half with a three-pointer, accompanied by a silly Mercer foul. The four-point play tied the game at 31–all. The crowd was in a frenzy as the teams exited the court. The Foxhounds had some momentum.

At the half, Darren made sure he told Tiffany he thought she was playing exceptionally well. Leadership at its best. Darren was slowly realizing that he could win by being emotionally stable and authentic with his team rather than the raging lunatic he once thought winning required. Tiffany's body language indicated the boost from her coach. A "great job" from the coach was all she needed.

The game ended in an 11-point victory—VCSU 69, Mercer 58. It was a total team effort. All five starters scored in double figures. The Foxhound Five held serve when their number was called. It was a perfect night. The jubilant Foxhounds were in first place at 1–0. Everyone in the locker room understood what had happened. The team, the program, and the people involved were sending notice to the Southern Conference that this team is no longer the pushover it once was.

Darren took to the front of the room and said joyously, "Ladies, I want to congratulate you on a superb effort. It was a total team effort and a win. Enjoy the night, but understand the work is not complete. Success is never final. We—and I say 'we' because this is what this team is becoming—we win more than I win. Great job, Coach Mays, Morris, Bennet, and Alexander. Everybody!"

Jimmy's text to Darren read, "*Congratulations! What a night for Foxhound basketball and the town of Eagle Gap. We are gaining on them. The team appears to be on track for a historic run. People are noticing, coming out, and buying gear. We're even getting some program donations. If we sold it, I'd buy stock in the Lady Foxhounds!*"

EMPATHY

> *The first step towards change is awareness.*
> *The second step is acceptance.*
>
> —Nathaniel Branden,
> Psychotherapist and Writer

✎ Darren ✎

They split the next six games, but the bar had been raised. With Vivian set to return and sitting at 4–3 in the conference and 10–9 overall, the Foxhounds seemed ready to push toward their first winning season in years. Adding Peck immediately added skill to the starting five, which consequently pushed Ruby back to her sixth-man role. Darren knew he needed to bring Ruby in to discuss Vivian's return and her move back to the bench to begin games.

"All leaders must be crystal clear in their communication," Jimmy stressed. "Be honest and upfront. It's the only way it will work. The truth is always acceptable."

Darren previously would have made the change without a conversation. But he was learning that communication was vital. Ruby needed to get the truth with a little extra care to gently guide her through this bump in the road.

As Ruby entered, Darren could tell she had an inkling of what was happening. Like he'd done before with Tiffany, he asked Ruby to walk with him. They didn't talk about basketball as they exited Lewis into the uncommonly warm mid-day air of late January. The students passing by wished him and Ruby luck at Wofford. One young lady stopped with her boyfriend for a photo of Ruby and the head coach. People were noticing and seemed genuinely excited about the women's team. The further they got from the building, talk easily transitioned to women's hoops.

"Would this have happened last year?" Darren asked. "You know, students wishing good luck, asking for autographs, and taking photos?"

"No way. Most days, we wouldn't even wear our gear. We were embarrassed. Nobody recognized us." She paused. "But it's different this year. Much more fun. It makes us feel good. I do, anyhow."

The walk took them to the university's deli. As they sat for lunch, Darren needed little time to resolve the issue. He did his best to soothe the pain of demoting a junior player with possibly the most talent on the team for a sophomore who had been out nearly a month. Darren knew it wasn't a unique experience for players; someone like Drew Bledsoe could sympathize with Ruby for sure.[3]

"I am proud of how much you have grown this year. You've been a real plus for us, and you have done nothing wrong. But with Vivian returning, our best team has you coming off the bench."

She nodded and took a deep breath—the kind you take before you do anything stressful to calm yourself. Darren could tell from her reaction that she was disappointed. He understood and empathized. Ruby sensed his genuine concern.

Darren decided now was a time for vulnerability. "When I was a senior, I was pulled as a starter for playing poorly and having a bad attitude. I was making bad decisions with the ball. My coach actually threw me out of practice for being a jerk to my teammates. He sat me two games. I hardly played. And we won without me. It was a tough time for me. But I got my attitude back on track, got back in, and helped the team."

Ruby was listening.

"You've done nothing wrong. And you will be playing, maybe more, coming off the bench. You are so freaking skilled! Starring in this sixth-man role is perfect for you and the team."

"I understand, Coach, and appreciate you being honest. A coach has never been so upfront with me. The past two years have been miserable. I wish you were here my freshman year. We all do. I would have been a better player. But I am glad you are here now."

Darren treasured the comments, justifying his newfound method of communicating negative news. He was gaining confidence in his interpersonal skills.

The Foxhounds arrived in Spartanburg with an air of confidence. At 4–3 in the conference, Darren's Foxhounds had notified anyone paying attention that this was not the VCSU team of the past. Still, Wofford would be a challenge. They were the highest-scoring team in the league, pushing to be the team to beat along with Chattanooga and East Tennessee, both of whom had beaten VCSU on their home turf. Wofford was eyeing a regular-season title.

The pace was fast at the tip—how fast? Blazing. Paul Westhead would have been proud.[4] Wofford pushed the ball up the court each time they had possession. The five-on-four, six-on-four practice drills, which disadvantaged defense, were paying off. Darren was a Bobby Knight guy. He used his concepts to better his teams, especially his defense.

On offense, Peck's ankle was holding up, but her lungs were not. Davis had to spell her multiple times throughout. Crowe's ability to handle the basketball enabled the team to break the press more than not. VCSU was handling Wofford's brand. Wofford, who averaged nearly 80 points per game, led by five 42–37 at the break. The break was a welcome sight. The Foxhounds were gasping.

The second half was more of the same. Wofford pressed and pushed all night, getting a shot off every 15 seconds. Crowe and company scratched and clawed to keep up. When the sound of the buzzer blasted to end the track meet, the dog-tired Foxhounds were left with an 81–75 hard-fought loss.

On the walk to the locker room, the unsatisfied Darren did his best to gather his thoughts and control his emotions. He wasn't bothered by the performance. He just hated to lose. His staff walked just ahead in silence. The Foxhounds were far ahead of expectations at 10–10 overall and 4–4 in the conference. Wofford did what they wanted when they wanted. They set the tempo from the get-go, and Darren's girls did little to slow the assault. Wofford was just better tonight.

The younger Coach Blood would have asked Wofford to keep the floor available for practice or called home to see if Lewis could be set up for a two-hour practice upon their arrival. He waited outside the locker room to gather himself. He felt the urge to be his old self. Losing still bothered him.

Darren walked directly to the center as he entered the muted locker room. He noticed dejection. Heads were hanging, and some had towels covering their faces. Misery was unmistakable. The team was visibly bothered.

"Hey, tonight, they were better. It happens sometimes." As he paused, looking across the room at the sad faces who were now all making eye contact, he said, "They have to come to us on the last weekend. We will be ready."

Darren's phone buzzed as he stepped onto the bus to return to Eagle Gap. It was Jimmy.

"Tough one tonight! We are right where we want to be with eight games remaining. You are doing a fantastic job. Call me if you need me. I will see you at the Pic & Pac in a few days. PS: Now, don't let these girls get comfortable. Remember, satisfaction is the death of success."

Even after the loss to Wofford, Darren was feeling the momentum, but there was danger as well.

FIGHTING COMPLACENCY

> *Complacency is the last hurdle standing between any team and its potential greatness.*
>
> —Pat Riley,
> NBA Hall of Fame Coach

✎ Darren ✐

The loss affected the team, and the coaches noticed it immediately. The next practice revealed sloppy fundamentals with below-the-standard enthusiasm. What was supposed to be 100 percent effort after crossing the Green Line was more like 60 percent. The coaches did their best to remain positive, pushing and teaching until, finally, the whistle sounded. Louder and longer than usual, Darren had seen enough. It was an unsettling scene.

As an NBA coach, Darren took what he saw as a bad practice and purposely made it worse. Throwing basketballs, kicking chairs, and occasionally ending practice by sending the players to the locker room with a verbal tirade. "I am sick of looking at this shit. You don't want it," he often said. Other times, he stared as if to say, "What the hell are you doing?" or would leave the practice floor and tell the team as he exited, "You f****** guys don't deserve to be coached."

It was only two days after the Wofford loss, and while it understandably stung, in Darren's eyes as their head coach, that was no excuse for the abysmal practice he was now forced to watch. The loss should have been a motivator to go even harder. It was as if they were satisfied where they were. Darren quickly questioned himself. Should he have been tougher on them after the loss instead of being overly positive?

Jimmy had once said to him, "Even the slightest amount of success is often too much to handle, especially for those who have never experienced success. It happens to everyone if you coach or play long enough. When you are not a consistent winner but begin to be the least bit successful, self-satisfaction becomes a mental barrier—a barrier that can set in and become a coach's nightmare." Darren knew it was time to apply this wisdom. Darren strolled toward the middle of the court with his head down. He felt his body trembling with anger, ready to implode, but was able to lasso his emotions and gain control. A few deep breaths later, Darren told the girls, "Bring it in." No one really moved. They knew their coach was upset. "Ladies, let's go," he said in a slightly louder voice. They jogged over.

For the next 10 seconds, he didn't say anything. The silence was deafening. "Months ago, when we came together, we decided what a true Foxhound player would look like. You decided. You did. Not me. Not the coaches. It was you," he said. "Do you remember what those qualities were?"

"Grit," Crowe said almost immediately.

"Excellence," Haley Boyles, one of the hardworking Foxhound Five, said.

Darren waited. "What else?

Tiana Wilson said, "Commitment."

"Yes, yes, yes!" said the animated head coach. Darren took the opportunity to give the team the truth. "But you know what? You know what, ladies? Today was the first time everyone was not at their best. None of you," he stressed as he panned the semi-circle team in front of him. "There was no evidence of excellence, commitment, and certainly no sign of grit. Yeah, we lost a tough one at Wofford, but that is what should motivate you to get back to work and get better. I don't like to lose, but it is the losses that get my motor going. To come out here with this attitude is not the culture we want. We need to be better than this." There was a moment of silence. It was clear that the entire team was locked in.

"There have been many examples of athletes and teams losing their momentum. They become complacent after a few wins and forget to work at the highest level to stay ahead of the competition. I remember one story from before you were born. In 1990, Mike Tyson was the undisputed heavyweight champion of the world. He was undefeated. He was considered indestructible. Invincible. Almost inhuman. No one stood a chance—no one. Until he fought a man named James 'Buster' Douglas. With odds at 42 to 1 to win, Douglas knocked Tyson out in the 10th round. It was Tyson's first loss. What happened? I think Tyson got a little complacent. He got a little too comfortable, and he paid the price. And it was one of the biggest upsets in sports history.[5]

"My point is that we cannot relax for one second. Not one second." Darren held up his index finger to punctuate the message. "Complacency is a human condition we fight every day. This goes for me too. We cannot be satisfied where we are." Darren's voice was stern but not loud. "Sure, there will be tough days. Days where you don't feel like being here. It doesn't matter, ladies. That is part of being a champion. You must work even when you don't feel like it. Is your commitment greater than your feelings? To be a champion, it has to be. You don't have a choice. We don't.

"Here is what we are going to do. You will all go back to the locker room, and I want you to come back when you're all ready to work at the standard we expect. As you cross that Green Line, you *will* be focused and ready to practice like a Foxhound. Remember, ladies, you don't *have* to play college basketball—you *get* to play college basketball. Let's refocus."

The team jogged back into the locker room. The staff hoped that vocal leaders Crowe and Peck would take charge, but the often overlooked Haley Boyles delivered the most impactful message.

"I work my ass off here. Every day. The coach wasn't talking about me out there. He was talkin' bout y'all. I know my role, and I'm okay with it, but c'mon! Even I could feel it. That was total bullshit." Her voice got louder with each word. "Do you remember last year? Huh? I do! It sucked. We got a real coach now. The AD loves us. People are coming to the games, and we are coming out like that today? Okay, so we lost to Wofford. We played our asses off. So what! So what we lost!" Exasperated and frustrated, Haley sat back down.

Crowe said, "Haley's right. Are we ready to go back out and practice like we're capable, or do you want me to tell coach we are not coming back out?"

No one uttered a word. Crowe then said, "Bring it in. We have one hour to bring it. Everybody in. All together now. 1-2-3, Hounds!"

They exited the locker room with a new and improved attitude. As each crossed the Green Line, it was overtly apparent practice was about to improve 100 percent. It did. Darren and his staff were smiling on the inside.

The final eight games would not determine *if* the VCSU women's basketball program had improved but rather by *how much* it had improved. It was the final exam for the evenly split 10-win, 10-loss Foxhounds. There would be more ahead for both the coach and the players, but they would overcome the obstacles to achieve ultimate success. Complacency was hopefully one of those obstacles they could flush from their system.

35 MENTAL IMAGERY

> *Any professional athlete will tell you that the mind is everything. For me, there is no shame in saying that I visualize and I meditate because it really works.*
>
> —Carli Lloyd,
> Olympic Gold Medalist

✎ Darren ✎

Darren knew that each practice, each meeting, each game was a means to an end. All part of the process. Jimmy had already told him that the season had exceeded expectations—not that he should ease off the gas pedal now. He and Jimmy were building a program that had a deep foundation in leadership, personal development, consistency, standards, expectations, a life-long learning mentality, and connecting with the right people. Darren, more of the right people were on the way. The coaches had already seen some promising high school seniors who showed interest in VCSU. Of course, they wouldn't know until we got them here if they would be able to perform at the required level. Would they show up each day to get better? Be a team-first player and make the tough choices?

The Foxhounds, sitting in fifth place, had a long week ahead of them: a four-day road trip starting in Birmingham, Alabama, and finishing in Macon, Georgia. Samford and Mercer were seeking redemption after losing to VCSU earlier in the season. Darren didn't let it bother him; he kept his head down, continued to teach, and tried to improve his game too. Jimmy had asked Darren in an earlier meeting how he'd rate his job performance this year. Darren had given himself a six overall, but even now, he knew that six was only possible because of the incredible team they'd transformed. He was never satisfied though. Losing motivated him, while winning was intoxicating—it was what had gotten him into trouble. He fought it every day. Thankfully, he now had Jimmy as his biggest supporter.

Every season is a journey. Teams, if coached well, continuously improve. Darren had one glaring concern: the ability to play well on the road. It was where they struggled, as indicated by the 1–3 in conference. Most young teams' goal is to conquer the road bug, but the Foxhounds hadn't quite managed that yet. To help with this trip, Jimmy had been kind enough to arrange for the team to leave a day earlier than usual—on a charter flight, no less. Darren saw yet another Jimmy lesson in action; he was caring for his people. Only then could they be situated to deliver the best results. Many leaders—bad leaders—fail to do this and often have short-lived success or no success at all.

The team had been at it since mid-October. Staying fresh was crucial. This was especially important for Darren to remember since he had a reputation for wearing down his team with extra-long practices and meetings. His staff was responsible for keeping tabs on the time they spent on the floor and in the meeting room to ensure he didn't go overboard.

In the past, Darren thought he had to do everything. That no one could do it better. Now, he delegated. All the help from his assistant coaches made the travel preparations easy. The team walked off the plane and onto the bus, looking first class. Another one of Darren's principles: Look good, play good. The Lulu swag helped.

Darren's pregame talk was low-key. He focused on two team fundamentals and Samford's star all-conference guard, Samantha Winters. "Take care of the basketball, get good shots, and make sure we keep the pressure on Winters. Take away their strength. In this case, it's Winters. Stop her, and you stop Samford." Peck was given the assignment to shut Winters down; she was ready for it.

From the start, Crowe took command on offense, leaving Peck to deal with Winters. The ball found Crowe every possession, and she made good each run down the floor. Her ability to see the floor was Magic Johnson-like, and her shot was tough to defend. Darren was proud—she was in the zone. The Wilson twins, Knoxy, and sixth man, Ruby Davis, got easy layups and short jumpers as a result of Samford's inability to guard the evasive Crowe. On the other end, Peck was making life for Winters a living hell. When Peck needed a breather, the athletic and much bigger Ruby Davis hounded Winters until her composure was tested. VCSU comfortably led at halftime, 40–29.

At the half, Darren was calm. There wasn't much left to say, so he reiterated, "Keep the pressure on Winters. Viv and Rube, you are kicking her butt. Don't let her breathe. Contest every shot on defense. Get a hand in her face. Continue to make things difficult. Let's finish strong and put this team away," said Darren to the team before they exited the locker room.

The second half began much like the game started. Crowe and Winters were doing their best to run their respective teams. Winters was frustrated all night by the tenacious Peck, who surrendered her normal position to help the team by handling Winter. There was no Peck to defend Crowe. She poured in 32 without a sweat as VCSU rolled 82–65 for only their second conference road win.

In the locker room, Darren addressed the team. "Let's understand what we did here tonight. We won *on the road* against a good team. You should be proud of yourself. Vivian Peck, you were outstanding. You shut their best player down. Trish Crowe, what can I say? You made everyone around you better. Everyone deserves credit for this one. It was a great team win." The team quieted as he paused and spanned the room. "But remember, this win will mean much more if we play well at Mercer too." He did his best not to say "win." He wanted to stay in process mode.

Darren continued, "What I want each of you to do on the four-hour ride to Macon is visualize yourself making great plays. Taking good shots with perfect form, playing unforgiving defense, boxing out, and making terrific passes. See yourself, see your teammates. Envision the crowd. Envision shutting down Mercer. Your mind does not know the difference. If you can see it, you can do it."

As the team boarded the bus for the drive to Macon, Darren's cell rang. It was Jimmy. "Nice job, Coach. You have them playing well. At the right time too."

"Thank you," said Darren. "There is a lot left, but we are coming together. The ladies seem to have accepted their roles. I'm proud of them."

"You should be. Travel safe. Talk to you later."

My friend, my boss, is nothing short of remarkable. I am lucky to have a guy in my corner. No one had ever cared for Darren on a professional level this much. Win or lose, Jimmy always called or sent a text because, having been a coach, he knew the value of someone supporting you in good times and bad.

As the bus pulled out from Samford, Crowe stood and said, "Let's visualize what we are going to do tomorrow. Like Coach said, 'If you can see it, you can do it.'" The team was locked in on their leader. "Be the best player on that floor." She turned and sat down.

Darren could hear Crowe, but neither he nor the assistant coaches turned their heads. Finally, she'd become the player's voice of the coaching staff. *Now, on to Mercer.*

Great leaders are always worried about what is next. This is why the greats *are* great. It is what's next that is most important. Leadership is always about the future.[6]

36 KAIZEN

> *If we can focus on making clear what parts of our day are within our control and what parts are not, we will not only be happier, we will have a distinct advantage over the other people who fail to realize they are fighting an unwinnable battle.*
>
> —Excerpt from *The Daily Stoic* by Ryan Holiday and Stephen Hanselman

⚔ Darren ⚔

Of course Gene Hack was not going to let them enjoy the win. Darren fought the urge to roll his eyes as he looked at the short story: "The Foxhounds may have found their coach for now, but history shows time is always the key ingredient. Can a coach with a reckless nature be sustainable? If you ask me, the answer is no. Darren Blood is not capable of controlling his emotions. It's a clear weakness. We all saw it in Chapel Hill. Externally, Blood-mania flourishes, but his weaknesses—that internal bleeding—will become visible with time. The nation can only sit back and wait. Eyes on you, Eagle Gap—and Darren Blood."

The Foxhounds were not bleeding internally. Anything but. The team completed the road sweep at Mercer with a 65–61 win. At 12–10, and 6–4 in the conference, the Lady Foxhounds could taste their first winning season in decades.

But the young team was still growing, and inconsistencies prevailed. The following four games proved it. It was lose one, win one, lose one, win one. Darren did his best to keep the team's confidence high, "We are still growing. And growing must include failure." Even so, he had let his emotions get the best of him during one of the home games. They'd been leading Chattanooga by one with less than two minutes remaining when a questionable foul was called on Knox. It looked like she had blocked a shot. The whistle blew, then Darren blew up. His obscenity-laced outburst led to an immediate technical foul. This was a crippling mistake, one that could not be overcome. There were two shots for the foul plus two shots and the ball for the technical. Their one-point lead instantly evaporated. VCSU suddenly trailed by six following a three-point goal. And Chattanooga left Eagle Gap like a thief in the night.

After the game, Darren was simmering in the locker room when Jimmy showed up. Darren was surprised by the gentle tone. *Jimmy must know I'm already beating myself up.* Instead of a dressing-down, Jimmy offered him some advice. "I know it is challenging. I lost my cool plenty of times. Then I learned to focus my energy on controlling what I can control. Anyone can unleash their anger—it takes a strong person to keep their composure when the seas are rough. Recognize your emotions. You're a high-energy guy, Darren, but you've done the work. Recognize the things that trigger you, then breathe, find your calm, and use it as a teaching point for the team."

Darren nodded and took a steadying breath as Jimmy continued, "Remember we discussed earlier this year how New York Yankee Aaron Judge clears his head. He resets during an at-bat by grabbing dirt and tossing it aside to signify that the pitch is over, that it is time to move ahead. That's what we need to do now. Throw the dirt to put this game in the past and focus on the next one." *It's always we, never you or me. He's the ultimate team player,* Darren thought before he responded.

"Yeah, I remember the Judge story. It's been working so far. I take a deep breath when I feel my emotions start to get the best of me, look down at the floor to gather myself, then I grab a drink of water. It has helped me so far. Tonight, I just let it get away. The call was bad, and I reacted poorly. It happened quickly. My response could have been better."

"We are all a work in progress," said Jimmy.

With the overall record at 14–12 and the conference record at 8–6, the next-to-last game at Western Carolina was their first opportunity to secure a winning season. They failed. The Catamounts rallied late, taking advantage of Foxhound turnovers and missed free throws to win a suspenseful 73–71 game. A loss like this can often send a team into a tailspin, especially a team so close to reaching a goal no one had ever experienced. Darren, who was becoming a read-the-room expert, stepped up to be a great leader for his team: getting to the positives, putting out the fires, and keeping the team focused on the final game that would determine whether or not this season would be a winning season. It was something Darren could have never done in his earlier years. That loss would have led to a torturous, negative lecture on failure, which would no doubt snowball into more lectures and even more defeats.

Darren walked slowly to the front of the room and began, "When the season began, no one gave us a chance. You have proven all of them wrong. It's not where you line up—it's where you wind up! And we will get the chance to show what we're made of this Saturday night. Here's our opportunity to put everything we've learned this year into 40 minutes of basketball. I have coached some of the best players in the world, and this year, you ladies and our coaches have taught me more about coaching and myself than I ever thought possible."

Darren paused as he was getting emotional. He continued, "It has been a wonderful season. But," he pointed his right index finger to the team, "we are not done yet. We have one more game to show the nation that our program is a contender, not a pretender." Darren saw determination set in. Everyone in the room was inspired. "We're ready for Wofford. Let's shake this off and keep our eye on Saturday."

The six-hour bus ride back to campus wasn't one of defeat. Darren could feel the team's energy as they focused ahead on their last game. They had two days to prepare for Saturday's final game of the season. Darren and his staff knew they had to make sure the team didn't overwork—staying fresh and ready to play their best game Saturday. It was all about what the Foxhounds would do. *We worry about what we do. We handle our business. It will not matter what the other team wants to do.*

On the final day of preparation, Darren only had one message before Friday's practice: "We dictate what happens Saturday night. We pressure them. We set the tempo. We focus and remain locked in. We play our best game."

The assistants took it from there. Crowe was her usual self—high energy, no BS. The two seniors, Hitchcock and Slade, who had struggled during the year, appeared to enjoy the work. *They're ready,* Darren thought. *Or, as ready as they can be.* He was proud the team had shaken off their Wednesday loss at

Western Carolina to focus on the final game of the season. The Foxhounds were at home, and The Lewis would be packed and loud with support. Their opponent, the Wofford Terriers, was talented and well-coached, but Darren hoped this challenge would bring out the best in his team. Most importantly, VCSU had a shot at a winning season and a first-ever fourth-place finish in the Southern Conference. They had pulled off the nearly impossible already. Gene Hack had to press pause on his smear campaign for now.

Wofford had plenty of incentive as well, needing the win to capture the regular-season championship and the number-one seed in the conference tournament. The prior 81–64 loss to Wofford still lingered in Darren's mind as they faced the biggest game of the year, VCSU's version of Duke versus North Carolina.

Senior Day at The Lewis had always been subdued. Usually, the season was in ruins, the crowd sparse, and the energy was just enough for a fan to remain vertical. This year was different. Jimmy had told Darren that each player would receive a framed jersey decorated with team and individual action photos. The team took to the court to honor their seniors, Tiffany Hitchcock and Dominique Slade. Not too long ago, the two players had been pariahs, energy drainers, and problems. Now, they were teammates, energy givers, and part of the solution. Most importantly, Darren and his coaches made them feel valued, a vital part of the program's transformation.

The crowd had grown slowly as the season progressed, and the final game was a sellout as fans flocked at the chance to see what many Eagle Gappers had never seen: a winning season for the Foxhounds.

Darren's pre-game talk was aimed at what he had preached earlier in the week: Pressure them, dictate tempo, be relentless on the boards, communicate on defense. Everything we have taught comes together tonight. The team took the floor, determined to pass this final test.

It was a departure from the norm. The Wilson twins and Knox were not in their usual positions in the frontcourt, and Peck and Crowe were in the backcourt. This was senior night, a night to honor the seniors Dominique Slade and Tiffany Hitchcock, who were playing alongside Peck, Crowe, and six-man Ruby Davis. For this final game, the lineup had come full circle, marking a significant moment in the season.

From the tip, Patricia Crowe brought the fury. As the extension of her head coach, she pushed the ball up and down the court. With constant penetration and pinpoint passing, she created easy layups for Hitchcock and Slade. Peck, now the team's second point guard, followed Crowe's lead. She, too, was exceptional in scoring from outside with her patented set shot. Wofford did not shy away from their aggressiveness. The Foxhounds were getting after the Terriers from Spartanburg, but the Terriers were not going away. They fought back, matching shot for shot. This up-and-down-the-court display put nearly 100 points on the scoreboard at the half: VCSU 48, Wofford 47.

As the coaches followed the team to the locker room, they paused for a quick exchange.

"Pretty good half. Real good, actually," Darren said. "So what did you see?"

"Our offensive has been tight. I'm not sure we can play any better there," said Coach Mays. The others agreed.

"Our defensive rebounding could use some work. They are outworking us down low and getting second and third shots," added Coach Bennet. Darren agreed.

"The pace is fast. We need to keep rotating our front line. Knox, the Wilsons, Tiffany, Dom, and Ruby need to be fresh. We can wear'em down," said Coach Morris.

"Anything else? Coach Alexander?"

"Get the ball to Crowe and get out of the way."

"That's sound advice, Coach." Nothing else was needed.

As Darren and his coaches entered the locker room, the energy hit them. Crowe was making rounds, fist-pumping her teammates. Peck followed with high fives. Even Tiffany was getting into the act, "Let's put this team away. Don't friggin let up."

Darren let them finish before stepping forward to speak. "Okay. That was a tremendous first half, ladies. Now, we have 20 more minutes of basketball." He paused, eyeing the room. "You need to continue that energy. It's not about X's and O's right now—it's all about attitude and effort." The girls nodded in agreement. "Let's hit the boards a little better. Don't give them those second and third shots. Be relentless. Find a body when the shot goes up. It's that simple. Let's finish this thing!"

The team put their hands in and cheered before jogging out to the courts. Darren followed behind with the other coaches. *It's time.* He couldn't help but feel nervous. It was the exciting kind of nervousness. He was enjoying coaching again.

Thankfully, the second half was a duplicate of the first. Crowe and Peck became one as the night continued. Darren smiled as he watched Wofford struggle to cover them. Conditioned like Iron Man competitors, they wore down the

Wofford guards. The Foxhounds scored at will. The Wilson twins were second-half warriors. Their game had taken not a step but a leap toward becoming bona fide DI players. Everyone was playing at the A-game level, 85 ability. Even the Foxhound Five looked like starters.

The close game vanished as Crowe and Peck hit their foul shots down the stretch, taking what was a nip-and-tucker to a 10-point win—VCSU 94, Wofford 84—guaranteeing that no matter what happened in the conference tournament, the Foxhounds could say they had a winning season. The fourth-place finish was their best since joining the conference. It was time to celebrate the win and the accomplishments tonight.

Darren took in the locker room scene: pure joy—the players, with beaming smiles, were a testament to the team's hard work and dedication. Seeing his players in such high spirits filled Darren with a happiness he never would have imagined. His bucket was overflowing.

"I am bursting with pride," he said. "Our players, coaches, trainers, and managers—you all played a crucial role in our journey to this moment. This season has been a learning curve for all of us. But you hung in, trusted the process, and battled when things were not in your favor. And you taught me so much about coaching along the way. I can confidently say this is one of the best nights I've ever had in my coaching career. Your performance was nothing short of magnificent. Congratulations. Enjoy this victory—you've earned it."

As the coach ended his talk, Patricia Crowe grabbed the metaphorical mic.

"Hey, hey," she shouted. Everyone calmed for a second. The room fell silent as Crowe spoke. "Coach, you have been a great leader, and we would not have accomplished any of this without you. Thank you, and for that, here is a game ball." Darren felt tears sting his eyes as the locker room cheered.

Darren looked over to Jimmy Harding, who had eased into the locker room unnoticed by the team, and smiled. "Ready for the next season?" Darren called over the noise to his president. The future was bright. *More meetings, coffee at the Pic & Pac, learning from his friend, and transforming into a great leader.* Darren had always known how to coach basketball, but he needed to learn how to lead. And it was Jimmy who took the chance. They'd made gains this year, but there was more to learn. There is always more to learn. *We are all a work in progress.* Darren wouldn't let go of his newly found growth mindset. They would step forward as a program, not backward. They would add, not subtract. Do the hard things. Ask others what they think. Darren would listen, be humble, and say thank you. He would encourage others to be their best and empower them. They were making improvements through small increments. It was kaizen at its best. Just as Jimmy had taught him.

It was the power of leading with emotional intelligence.

SUMMARY OF PART IV:
THE CONFERENCE SEASON

1. **Take Your One-on-One Meetings Outside of Your Office**

   Changing the environment for one-on-one meetings can foster more open, relaxed conversations. Walking meetings, in particular, reduce stress and allow for clearer thinking, encouraging a more productive and candid exchange. It's an effective way to build rapport and open communication lines with your team.

2. **Be the Never-Shaken Leader**

   In athletics and leadership, emotional control is crucial. The most successful leaders stay composed and never let external challenges shake their confidence or decision-making. Always model calmness, confidence, and resilience for your team.

3. **Be an Empathetic Leader**

   Great leaders put themselves in the shoes of others, creating an environment where people feel valued. Empathetic leaders build trust and a comfortable level of communication—people should feel like their coach/boss truly understands them. This level of understanding creates stronger connections and loyalty.

4. **Avoid Complacency**

   Complacency is the enemy of progress. Always remember that success is never final. The best leaders avoid overconfidence, staying hungry for growth and improvement. A mindset that says, "I haven't made it yet," keeps you focused, driven, and on course for long-term success.

5. **Have an Attitude of Excellence**

   Attitude often outweighs talent in leadership. Leaders who prioritize a positive, growth-oriented attitude attract talented people who share that mindset. Great leaders search for individuals with a can-do attitude who exhibit resilience in the face of adversity. It's not just about skills; it's about how you approach challenges. After all, how you do anything is how you do everything (HUDA HUDE).

6. **Be Self-Reflective**

   Leaders should reflect regularly—daily, weekly, monthly, and annually. Honest self-reflection helps you identify your strengths and, more importantly, areas for improvement. By reviewing your performance and actions, you can better understand how to grow as a leader and refine your approach to challenges.

7. **Kaizen Is Improvement in Small Increments**

   Great leadership isn't about quick fixes. It requires consistent effort, self-discipline, and a commitment to choosing hard work over shortcuts. Successful leaders seek to improve themselves daily—striving for that 1 percent improvement or the +1 mindset. I will be better today than yesterday and better tomorrow than I am today.

A SUMMARY ON EMOTIONAL INTELLIGENCE

There are five components to emotional intelligence (EQ):

➲ Self-Awareness: understanding your mood and responding appropriately

➲ Self-Regulation: understanding and controlling your emotions

➲ Motivation: the grit and perseverance to stay on task

➲ Empathy: listening and closely relating to other people's emotions

➲ Social Awareness: i.e., people skills[7]

Dan Goleman, the father of emotional intelligence, says:

"Self-absorption in all its forms kills empathy, let alone compassion. When we focus on ourselves, our world contracts as our problems and preoccupations loom large. But when we focus on others, our world expands. Our own problems drift to the periphery of the mind and so seem smaller, and we increase our capacity for connection—or compassionate action.[8]

"We're being judged by a new yardstick: not just by how smart we are, or by our training and expertise, but also by how well we handle ourselves and each other. In short, out-of-control emotions can make smart people stupid."[9]

Author Coach Barry Davis, PhD, says:

"Emotional intelligence is what separates average leaders from elite ones; to be a great leader, you must understand your emotions and, more importantly, the emotions of others."

PART IV
REFERENCES

1. "A Football Life: Mean Joe Greene," posted October 24, 2023, YouTube, 44 min., 35 sec., https://www.youtube.com/watch?v=ZFfe9c6d9Tg.
2. "Twin Towers on the Rise," *Sports Illustrated,* November 3, 1986.
3. Justin Leger, "Drew Bledsoe Reflects on Losing Job to Tom Brady in 2001: 'A Tough Pill to Swallow,'" NBC Sports Boston, February 10, 2020, https://www.nbcsportsboston.com/nfl/new-england-patriots/drew-bledsoe-reflects-on-losing-job-to-tom-brady-in-2001-a-tough-pill-to-swallow/381871/.
4. "Westhead: His Team's Always in the Running," *Chicago Tribune,* December 18, 1988, https://www.chicagotribune.com/1988/12/18/westhead-his-teams-always-in-the-running/.
5. James Sterngold, "No Heart? Douglas Disproves Doubters," *New York Times,* February 12, 1990, https://www.nytimes.com/1990/02/12/sports/no-heart-douglas-disproves-doubters.html.
6. Pat Williams, lecture, ABCA Convention, Orlando, Florida, 2007.
7. Daniel Goleman, *Emotional Intelligence: Why It Can Matter More Than IQ* (Bloomsbury, 1996).
8. Daniel Goleman, *Social Intelligence: The New Science of Human Relationships* (Bantam Books, 2007).
9. Daniel Goleman, *Working with Emotional Intelligence* (Bantam Books, 1998).

The story of Virginia Central State University's women's basketball program is an all-too-familiar one: a struggling athletic program that has never truly experienced success and now finds itself a doormat in the rapidly growing world of women's basketball. In a win-now climate, university stakeholders have made it clear—failure is a habit they will no longer accept. The only path forward is to make a change in leadership.

The primary factor in making any change in athletics or business is the bottom line. In athletics specifically, it often comes down to too many L's and not enough W's. In today's collegiate environment, the so-called five-year plan for coaches has completely vanished. Now, it's all about immediate results. Virginia Central State University had waited long enough to get theirs. A leadership shakeup at the presidential level paved the way for a new head coach.

The selection of head coaches is arguably the most critical decision university leaders will make for their athletic programs. Yet, the success rate is alarmingly inconsistent. Universities are spending enormous amounts of money on coaches who are not actively coaching. This phenomenon, referred to as "dead money," has exceeded half a billion dollars over the past decade. Why is this process such an inexact science? My hypothesis: Leaders only conduct surface-level searches for the head coach who fits best, resulting in too many swings and misses.

The selection process for a head coach should consider five pressure-treated and time-tested pillars. The key is that all five must be present to transform and sustain success on the field or court. These five key pillars include leadership and leadership development, consistency and consistent communication, high standards, the right fit, and a growth mindset.

However, there is a sixth pillar that serves as the game changer—emotional intelligence. Emotionally intelligent coaches have a distinct advantage over those who lack this skill. Research has shown that organizations led by individuals with high emotional intelligence (EQ) are more successful than those without it. Those who possess EQ are more aware and in control of their emotions while also being empathetic and socially aware of others. A competent coach who can control his emotions at the height of adversity while demonstrating excellent people skills will win more.

This fictional account of a season with the Lady Foxhounds illustrates how developing emotional intelligence is vital for maximizing one's and others' potential. The interpersonal skills demonstrated in this story serve as a model for implementing emotional intelligence in coaching and leadership. Investing in the mentorship of our team members is crucial for leadership development, requiring both time and patience.

In *Old Dog, New Tricks*, I aimed to showcase, through real-life experiences, how an athletic program or organization can be transformed and sustained for long-term success. With an open mind, a willingness to embrace change, and guidance from a mentor, we can all transform ourselves and others to achieve our best and, in turn, our team's best.

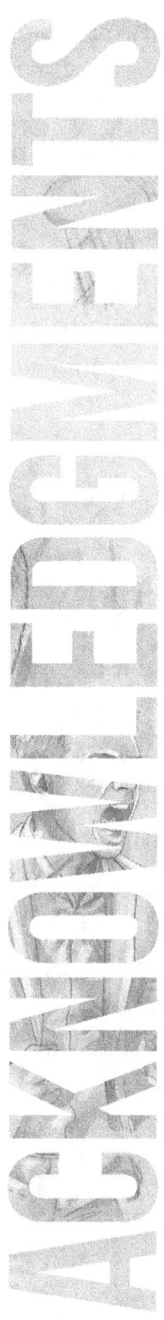

I am incredibly grateful to my wife, Brett Ashley, who has supported me throughout this process. You encouraged me to follow my dream of writing a book, you provided guidance and advice when I needed it the most, and you pushed me when it became a challenge to rise on those early morning days. If I ever needed help with writing or making tough decisions, you were there with the answer. None of this is possible without you. And you are among the most intelligent and determined people I have ever met. I love you dearly and cannot travel life's path without you.

Thank you, Buddy, our Cavalier King Charles Spaniel, for teaching me patience. Your presence is always comforting. It has kept me grounded, keeping the most important things the most important things. Any challenge I have encountered is much easier knowing you were there with that look of love and need. Our walks gave me time to reflect and get better.

Thank you, Mom and Dad, for supporting me my entire life. You never pushed me, but you were always there to cheer me on, encourage me to follow my heart, and be the best at whatever I chose.

Thank You, Grandaddy and Grandma. Your love was immeasurable. You never missed a game. Never. Your support was unwavering. It was always comforting to see you in the stands watching.

Thank you to my only brother. You have supported my efforts and have been there when I and the family needed you.

Thank you to my kids, Derek and Amanda. Although coaching took me away from you many days and nights, you were always understanding. You backed and defended me when I needed you most. I love you both.

Thank you to the hundreds of players. You bought into a tough, loving style of coaching and excelled. You taught me more than you can imagine, and if not for you, there would not have been a championship to celebrate.

Thank you, Neil Leake, Ray Bates, and Bruce Maxa. As my youth coaches, you made me feel good about myself. You made it fun to play baseball and made me want to do more.

Thank you, Coach Carrol Bickers, for always being interested in helping me become a better player. You encouraged me to read about the game and learn more about how to play.

Thank you, Donnie Wright. As my high school coach, you pushed me, coached me, and showed me how to become a better player. You trusted me and made me feel important. You are a big reason I am who I am.

To my college coaches, Dr. Tom Kinder and Curt Kendall, thank you. Dr. Kinder, you wanted me to be the best I could be. You never wavered on the discipline required to be a good person. Curt Kendall, you allowed me to be me. You gave me the courage to lead others. My coaching interest came from playing for you. You made me want to coach at the collegiate level.

Thank you to my coaching colleagues who have shared their knowledge, worked with me, and competed against me. I am a better coach because of all of you.

Thank you to the Bridgewater College community. It is where I gained the confidence I never had. My four-year experience led me to a future in leadership. My professors taught me how to be a teacher, and my teaching skills are a direct result of their knowledge and experience in education.

Thank you, Coach Billy Brown, better known to many as "Skip," but you will always be Coach Brown to me. I appreciate your willingness to allow a young 22-year-old me to become an assistant coach at George Mason University. You taught me how to lead young people and organize and run a baseball program. I won a lot of games because of you. No one else is responsible for giving me a start in my life's journey.

Thank you, Coach Bob Wells. While at Frostburg State University, you inspired me to think deeper than I was ever asked to think. As a coach, no one was as good as you at running a game. I won a lot of games because you taught me how to teach and think about the game. As an author, you inspired me to be a writer. If I become half the writer you are, I will be fulfilled.

Thank you, Dr. Rob Gilbert, for stimulating me to think outside of the box. This story can be attributed to your creative thinking. You showed me how to be positive and remain positive when things get tough. You are one of the best at making others believe they can do more than they thought capable.

Thank you, Brian Cain, for motivating and inspiring me to take on and complete this project. The very idea that I could do this can be traced directly to your "dominate the day" attitude. You believed in it, and I'm grateful for your guidance.

And a final thank you to the BrightRay Publishing team. To Warren Wilkes for initially reaching out to me about collaborating on a book project—your timing was impeccable. Thank you to Emily McBatdorf and Zoe Rose for your expertise and patience in working with a first-time author. This book would not be possible without your efforts.

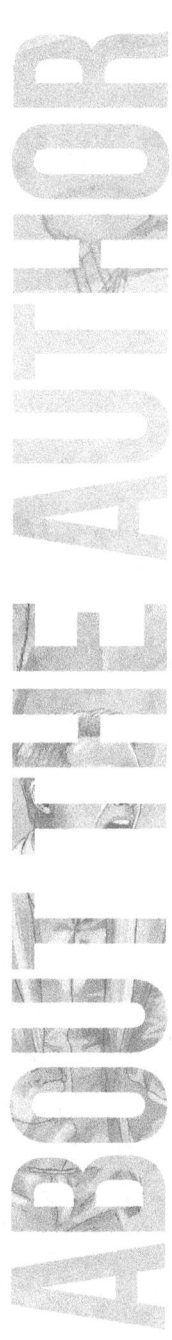

Coach Barry Davis, PhD, is a prominent head college baseball coach of 35 years, a leadership consultant, and a keynote speaker. As a head baseball coach, he led his teams to four DIII Junior College National Championships, six Metro Atlantic Athletic Conference Championships, and four NCAA Regional Tournament appearances. Recognized nationally for his ability to transform and build championship cultures, Davis has revitalized three baseball programs and achieved a remarkable total of 1,054 wins. He is a seven-time Coach of the Year and has been inducted into five Hall of Fames.

Coach Barry Davis uncovered the hidden driver of excellence—emotional intelligence—during his groundbreaking research for his dissertation. Through this work, he identified five key pillars that transformed struggling programs into perennial winners. However, even the strongest program cannot sustain excellence without a leader who masters emotional intelligence.

Davis now assists leaders from various fields—coaches, executives, and anyone looking to elevate their leadership skills—by helping them develop the tools to lead with empathy, manage emotions effectively, and create environments conducive to success.

Davis earned a PhD in sports leadership from Concordia University Chicago, a master's degree in education from Frostburg State

University, and a bachelor's degree in health and physical education from Bridgewater College.

Coach Davis lives in Langhorne, PA, with his wife, Brett, and their dog, Buddy.

www.ingramcontent.com/pod-product-compliance
Lightning Source LLC
Chambersburg PA
CBHW061145120626
46546CB00005B/1937